Living in Victory

8 Spiritual Truths for Transformation and Renewal

Joel Comiskey, Ph.D.

JOEL COMISKEY GROUP RESOURCING THE WORLDWIDE CELL CHURCH

Published by CCS Publishing
23890 Brittlebush Circle
Moreno Valley, CA 92557 USA
1-888-511-9995

Cover design by Jason Klanderud
Editing by Scott Boren, Lee Warren, and Jay Stanwood

ISBN: 978-1-950069-01-9
LCCN: 2019915201

CCS Publishing is the book-publishing division of Joel Comiskey Group, a resource and coaching ministry dedicated to equipping leaders for cell-based ministry.
Find us on the World Wide Web at **www.joelcomiskeygroup.com**

Contents

Praises

This is Joel Comiskey's most intimate book. The accumulation of experiences and knowledge acquired throughout his life are generously and sincerely brought out in this book. They are the keys to a balanced and victorious life. Each of them has been a pivotal part of Joel's life, and he writes from years of experience. The proposal is that an integral spirituality that starts from the sovereignty and grace of God will also reach down into our need for rest, taking care of our bodies, families, and church life. Comiskey believes that a balanced life provides the foundations for living in victory. I recommend this book for all Christians, but especially for small group leaders and coaches. Pastors will also greatly benefit as they plan a long life of service to God *(Mario Vega, lead pastor of the Elim church, San Salvador, El Salvador)*

Joel Comiskey provides 8 simple, clear, and biblical principles that will help you live a victorious Christian life. Dr. Comiskey does not just write about theoretical truths. Rather, he has tested these principles in his own life and attempts to live by them daily. In this book, Comiskey writes about God's sovereignty, grace, spending daily time with God, relationships, the local church, rest, taking care of your body, and preparing for eternity. Read this book if you are looking to grow in your relationship with Jesus *(Aluizio Silva, founder and lead pastor of the Vine Church [Videira] in Brazil)*

In *Living in Victory*, Joel shares from first-hand experience the importance of tapping into the enduring, classic sources of a well-ordered life. Whether you are new to spiritual disciplines or a veteran practitioner, there is wisdom and strength here for all who apply what he teaches (*Dr. Steve Cordle, Lead Pastor, Crossroads Church, Pittsburgh and author of "The Church in Many Houses" and "A Jesus-Shaped Life"*)

Why do so many people who attend church lack the joy, inner peace, and clear vision that Jesus came to bring? Joel Comiskey, in an extraordinary way, answers this question. This book provides a clear, practical analysis of key principles that will help a person live in victory, while avoiding the frustration of not experiencing the abundant life that God has for each servant! I believe that God will use this book as a bridge to spiritual maturity, even in the face of struggles and obstacles that knock at the door of each believer (*Josué Valandro de Oliveira Jr, founder and lead pastor of Attitude Church, Rio de Janeiro, Brazil*)

Acknowledgements

I'm very grateful to Jay Stanwood for carefully reading over this manuscript. He helped me untangle unclear sentences while suggesting better ways to say the same thing. Jay also recommended additional Scripture references, the need to combine specific paragraphs, and insightfully guided me to move a complicated table from the main body of the book to the appendix. The final product is much better because of Jay Stanwood's help.

Scott Boren, my primary editor, helped me to understand the main theme of this book. Boren excels at challenging my logic and bringing the chapters in line with the book's essence: *Living in Victory*. This book now fits together because Scott Boren strongly critiqued the early drafts to bring the chapters together into a unified whole.

I'm also thankful to Lee Warren, my copyeditor, for offering many valuable corrections and suggestions and even updating all Scripture references to the latest NIV version.

My cover designer, Jason Klanderud, was very gracious in going through multiple cover revisions to finally find the one that fit the spirit of this book. I appreciate his flexibility, expertise, and persistence to work with me to find the right cover.

Introduction

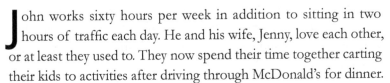

John works sixty hours per week in addition to sitting in two hours of traffic each day. He and his wife, Jenny, love each other, or at least they used to. They now spend their time together carting their kids to activities after driving through McDonald's for dinner.

Every week, John sits in the second row at church, listening to the pastor, and he and Jenny volunteer in children's church. But John is exhausted. On the surface, he has the good life, but deep down, he is drowning. He has no real victory.

Years ago, John was more involved in the church. He went to multiple Christian conferences, participated on mission trips, and even started a small group in his home. But then he began to feel distant from God due to his increasingly busy schedule. He struggled with having a daily quiet time, even though he tried repeatedly, especially after his pastor preached on the topic. John does pray on the way to work and sometimes during the day, but lately, those prayers have been his nourishment. But he hasn't found time to go to one of the midweek home groups the church offers.

John is increasingly worn out. His weight has increased, which worries him. *I'll renew my gym membership and lose weight*, he often tells himself. Over-eating has become a subconscious way to ease his exhaustion, but he's also noticing more serious problems, like shortness of breath. "Should I go to the doctor?" he recently asked Jenny. *I just don't want to spend the extra money.*

Jenny has patiently insisted for years that they take a day off, but John feels guilty unless he's working. "My boss insists that I work on Saturday," he recently told her. "And on Sunday, you go to your mom's house."

John tries to do what is right but feels increasingly guilty, like he should be doing more for God. *But what? Should I talk to the pastor? I probably should tell him about our marriage problems.*

John needs victory. But what can he do? How does someone like John stem the tide? Where does he start? Many find the answer in promises of a magic pill, something that provides a quick fix. But such fixes don't exist. The victory of God is an ongoing lifestyle of adopting and applying certain priorities that prepare and equip one for life.

Tammy, unlike John, is new to Christianity. She accepted Jesus one year ago while visiting a large megachurch in the area. She was desperate for answers after experiencing a divorce. She started well but soon found it difficult to connect with others. The church just seemed too large, so she stopped going. She knows she should try again, but with the resistance of her two adolescent sons, she feels as though she is swimming upstream. *What am I going to do when they start asking questions about faith?* she often asks herself. She will sometimes pick up her Bible, watch TV preachers, and even occasionally make it to the Sunday service.

Tammy struggles with impatience that quickly leads to anger as she tries to discipline her two teens. She fears her kids are becoming bitter. Lately, she's become more desperate as her teens come home from school wanting to hang out with new friends. *They are becoming independent so quickly.* She worries about their future as she sees so much violence and corruption on the news.

Tammy does have a vague idea of what Christian victory might look like as she has observed her brother Tom's happy marriage, good job, and consistent walk with Jesus. But she doesn't have a close relationship with Tom and is hesitant to confide in him.

Tammy has noticed that Mary, her work associate and valued part of the company, often talks about Jesus and even attributes her success in marriage to her walk with God. *Should I approach Mary for counsel?* Tammy believes victory is possible but just doesn't know how to make it happen.

Many people, like John and Tammy, need victory in their Christian lives. They have accepted Jesus but are not walking in the abundant life that God has for them. God, in fact, wants all of us to experience victory in our Christian lives. But the victory of God is not a one-time thing. Rather, it's a journey that leads through good and bad times. More than an event; it's a lifestyle.

Perhaps you're reading this book because you desire more from God. Perhaps at one time you experienced the victory that you now long for. Or maybe you've seen this victory in a close friend or family member. You want what he or she has.

Several years ago, I gave a seminar in a growing church in Fort Worth, Texas. The pastor asked me to share the passions and principles that guide my own life. He wanted his congregation to hear the values that made Joel Comiskey tick, and the truths that helped me live victoriously.

As I thought about it, I noticed that victory in my own life came from the difficult trials that led me to go deeper with God and Scripture. The truths that God burned into my soul came through the anvil of hard knocks and tough experiences. The passions and principles I share in the pages of this book have come from my study of Scripture as I've dealt with obstacles and challenging circumstances. I think of my own need for:

- Believing that God was really in control of all things (chapter 1). During periods when my life seemed random and out of control, I learned to lean hard on God's sovereignty. I remember the weeks visiting my wife in the hospital when I felt confused and frustrated. My only refuge was God and the knowledge that he was in control of all things. God's sovereign control has given me confidence and victory to believe that he does know the way, and I can trust in him.

- Grace (chapter 2). I've been learning that trying to please God by my own good works leads to more guilt and less freedom. Turning to grace and God's love were the only solutions. Faith in what Jesus has done for me on the cross has given me new freedom and victory. God's grace and love have become my refuge and hope.

- Spending time with God (chapter 3). How often have I tried to enter my day without God's presence and guiding hand? I've quickly realized that I lacked the strength and vitality, feeling irritated and directionless. I've learned from experience that I need to have a daily quiet time, to feed on God's Word, receive the Spirit's filling, and especially to know him more intimately.

- Relationships (chapter 4). As an individualist and achiever, I've often assumed that God was primarily concerned with what I accomplished for him. God has taught me that he is a relational God and wants me to have successful relationships with those I'm closest to. My true Christian walk and lifestyle is revealed and tested by those who know me best. He wants me to prioritize relationships on a deeper level and to realize that true success is practicing the Christian life with those who I'm closest to.

- Family of God (chapter 5). God has rescued me from false doctrine and spiritual error on more than one occasion. During those moments, God used local church pastors to guide me into biblical truth. I've also realized my need for participation in a small group where I can share my own struggles and hear others share theirs. An important part of confidence and victory is connecting with a local church and growing with the family of God over time.

- Rest (chapter 6). Through sickness and burnout, God has shown me the need to prioritize rest. I have often wanted to accomplish one more thing for God only to hear him tell me that he was more concerned about me. He wanted me to rest. God has repeatedly shown me the need for rest, both on a weekly basis and through extended vacation times. I've learned that I can accomplish much more when I'm rested and alert.

- Care for my body (chapter 7). During times of poor health through neglecting my body, God has revealed key principles that lead to victory. I used to think it was okay to get as little sleep as possible. Not anymore. God has wired each of us to operate better with enough sleep, proper nutrition, and consistent exercise. God is concerned about the body he has given us.

- Keeping the end in view (chapter 8). I've wanted jobs and promotions that God didn't want for me. I had one person in mind: Joel Comiskey. God graciously directed me to remember that true riches are in the next world. True victory is living for God and preparing for eternity. I've had to ask him to keep my eyes on the eternal reward that he graciously offers.

Over the years, God has branded these priorities on my soul through the school of hard knocks. He's also given me greater victory through them.

But this book is not primarily about me. Most of the principles in this book form the body of literature called the *Christian disciplines* or *spiritual disciplines*. In other words, men and women of God for the last 2,000 years have learned to walk in victory through practicing similar disciplines and principles. I've drawn from these men and women in the pages of this book. There's nothing new under the sun, and I've had to lean heavily on the experience of others while writing this book.

I haven't arrived, and no one ever will. Complete victory takes place in heaven, not here on earth. But I am growing in Jesus as I practice these principles. My prayer is that Jesus will empower you to live in victory as you read and practice what is written in this book.

Trust That God Is in Control

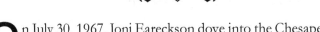

On July 30, 1967, Joni Eareckson dove into the Chesapeake Bay after misjudging the shallowness of the water. She suffered a fracture between the fourth and fifth cervical levels and became a quadriplegic, paralyzed from the shoulders down.

As she lay in the hospital, she knew she was facing a lifetime of severe hardship and disability. She also knew she was going to be a burden on others who would have to take care of her. Day after day, Joni contemplated the ultimate questions of life: Does God exist? If God does exist, does He care? What is the purpose of life? Joni concluded that if there was no God, the most logical thing to do was to kill herself. Not only would suicide end her pain and misery, but it would also relieve the people she loved of the tremendous burden her disability had put on them.

Even in the depths of her despair, Joni could not shake the belief that her life, and the life of every human being, has significant meaning and purpose. With that hope in mind, Joni began a long process of rehabilitation. During her two-year stay at the hospital, Joni learned to paint by holding a brush in her mouth, how to get her arms to move a little by utilizing her back muscles, and how to live as independently as possible in her wheelchair.

Since her accident, Joni has achieved more than most people could imagine. She has become an accomplished artist, writer, musician, and founder of the Joni and Friends, a ministry that has reached millions. What is her secret? She has trusted God to use her terrible predicament to give hope to millions. She has allowed

God to restore her broken dreams and bring good out of a terrible situation. At the time of this writing, Joni has spent fifty-three years in a wheelchair as a quadriplegic. She has learned things about God and his purposes that are "*so* satisfying" and "*so* pleasurable," that she "wouldn't trade the wheelchair for anything!"[1]

Joni doesn't believe that what happened to her was an accident. Rather, God was in charge and has sovereignly guided her to this moment. She's learned to live in victory as she depends on the living God for her support and strength. She is the first to admit that she's weak. She often talks about how hard it is to get out of bed or to speak at a conference. But she realizes that God is using her weakness to receive all the glory.

Who Is in Charge?

Many people do not believe that God is in control of their lives. They think they are the captains of their own ship and really don't have a need for God. Others believe that God might exist but that he's not actively involved in their personal affairs or the affairs of the world. It's a subtle form of deism—the belief that God wound up the clock and then let it tick down. According to this view, God started the process when he created the world, but then he just allows things to happen naturally without any guidance or influence.

Most people still believe in moral standards but not in a God who is actively involved in their lives. Evolution, not God as Creator, has become standard teaching in many classrooms around the world. According to this theory, all creatures evolved from a series of adaptations and random errors that occurred over eons of time. Time and chance resulted in the creation of all living creatures, including human beings according to evolution theory. All of life, therefore, is random and purposeless without a Creator. Birth is an accident and our lives don't exist after death.

Scripture, on the other hand, tells us that God, the Creator, is actively involved in all his Creation. Paul said, "For by him all things were created: things in heaven and on the earth, visible and invisible, whether thrones or powers or rulers or authorities; all things were created by him and for him" (Colossians 1:16). Trusting in God's providence or sovereignty gives us victory in the Christian life.

God Is Actively Involved

In July 2002, I was tired and frustrated. I had written a devotional book that I envisioned would be a bestseller. I had worked so hard not only to write the book but also to market it and land an important TV spot that went beyond the publisher's own marketing plan. I was convinced that the book would be a runaway hit. It wasn't. We, as a family, had just arrived in California after eleven years in Ecuador. Life was different and difficult as we adjusted to another cultural experience. I longed for our life in Ecuador, and then the book sales began to fizzle. As the sales trickled off, I became increasingly tired and discouraged.

I was attending my wife's family camp, and I really didn't want to meet other people. I was just too tired and forlorn. It was then I remembered a systematic theology course I'd taken in which I learned about God's sovereign control or providence. I remembered how much this biblical theme soothed me back then, and I realized I needed to know God was in control in this moment.

I began to meditate on God's sovereignty, believing God was guiding my life, actions, and even thoughts. I was too tired to do otherwise. *God, can you guide me to the table where I will eat and meet the people I should talk with? I just don't have the energy to plan out my schedule,* I prayed. As I began to trust God, I felt a peace, assurance, and victory. I was no longer worried about who I talked with or what I said. I left those details to God. I could rest in his love for me. Proverbs 3:5–6 took on new meaning, "Trust in the Lord with all your heart and lean not on your own understanding; in all your ways submit to him, and he will make your paths straight." I prayed, *God, I want to commit myself to your control from this day onward. I don't want to worry about all the details of my life. I'm going to trust that you have it all planned out. I'm going to rest in you.*

Out of that dark time period, I put a stake in the ground to trust God's sovereign control. I began to journal continually about God's providential participation in every aspect of my life. The journaling grew into a large document, from which I began to meditate daily. I noticed a new confidence and victory in my life as I trusted him to lead me step by step, believing that he was in control of all things.

God's sovereignty should give us hope. Victory comes as we comprehend that God knows, cares about, and guides our lives through our circumstances. The psalmist declares:

> I know that the LORD is great, that our Lord is greater than all gods. The LORD does whatever pleases him, in the heavens and on the earth, in the seas and all their depths. He makes clouds rise from the ends of the earth; he sends lightning with the rain and brings out the wind from his storehouses (Psalm 135:5–7).

In this life, nothing escapes his tender loving care. God knows the beginning, the end, and everything in between. Often I wonder, *Where am I heading right now and am I in the right place?* I cannot see how the circumstances fit together. Life seems random and out of control. In such times I come back continually to the truth of God's loving providence and guidance.

I enjoy watching the sparrows in my backyard. They are common birds, unlike hummingbirds or woodpeckers. Yet, even a sparrow doesn't escape the heavenly Father's attention. Jesus said, "Are not five sparrows sold for two pennies? Yet not one of them is forgotten by God. Indeed, the very hairs of your head are all numbered. Don't be afraid; you are worth more than many sparrows" (Luke 12:6–7). Jerry Bridges writes,

> God does exercise His sovereignty in very minute events—even in the life and death of a little sparrow. And Jesus' whole point is: If God so exercises His sovereignty in regard to sparrows, He will most certainly exercise it in regard to His children.[2]

Humans are the crown of God's creation, and he values every aspect of their lives. Listen to how David describes God's love and intimacy for his creation,

> My frame was not hidden from you when I was made in the secret place, when I was woven together in the depths of the earth. Your eyes saw my unformed body; all the days ordained for me were written in your book before one of them came to be. How precious to me are your thoughts, God! How vast is the sum of them! Were I to count them, they would outnumber the grains of sand—when I awake, I am still with you. (Psalm 139:15–18)

In the Scriptures, God says, "Do not be afraid, little flock, for your Father has been pleased to give you the kingdom" (Luke 12:32). He doesn't want us to toil, sweat, and try to figure it out on our own. Jesus said in Matthew 11:28–30, "Come to me, all you who are weary and burdened, and I will give you rest. Take my yoke upon you and learn from me, for I am gentle and humble in heart, and you will find rest for your souls. For my yoke is easy and my burden is light." Victory comes in knowing that we can trust his sovereign will.

Even when life seems like it is out of control and impossible, we know that God is all-powerful and can change the current circumstances—and he often does. Scripture tells us that he's able to do immeasurably more than all we ask or imagine (Ephesians 3:20). How? Because of his divine power working in us and through us (Ephesians 3:20). Trusting God's sovereignty is a daily challenge of believing God and resisting the natural doubt that prompts us to believe we must figure everything out.

The much-loved verse in Romans 8:28 should be our guiding light, "And we know that in all things God works for the good of those who love him." God is guiding and directing all things so that he fulfills his plan for our lives. He has the best possible outcome for us in mind. Our own comprehension is faulty and limited. But the God of the universe sees each circumstance, and he knows how that problem will benefit us. We can rest and even relax when we know that God is guiding us through our circumstances.

God even takes our failures and uses them for his glory and our good. The prophet Jeremiah describes our lives as clay in a potter's hand (Jeremiah 18). We start out unformed, but the potter knows what he is creating and forming. And even if the pot is marred or broken, the potter can make a brand-new vessel, something even better. Likewise, God takes the mistakes and defects and uses them to benefit us. Granted, during trials and hardships, it's difficult to understand the potter's intention, but Scripture over and over tells us we can trust a loving, caring God who has a perfect plan for us.

Hannah, a woman in the Old Testament who had trouble getting pregnant, didn't realize that God had a plan for her unborn child. Hannah experienced pain, and even shame, for not having a child. God used the period of waiting and suffering to bring Hannah to the point of dedicating her son, Samuel, to God's service. In her state of anxiety, she cried out to God and he answered. Hannah's son, Samuel, became one of the greatest prophets of the Old Testament. Later she said, "The Lord brings death and makes alive; he brings down to the grave and raises up. The Lord sends poverty and wealth; he humbles and he exalts" (1 Samuel 2:6–7).

God's sovereignty goes all the way back to our genes, those intimate combinations that God had planned before the creation of the world. Notice how Paul describes his wonderful plan for us, "In him we were also chosen, having been predestined according to the plan of him who works out everything in conformity with the purpose of his will" (Ephesians 1:11).

God Rules the Nations

One of the greatest Roman emperors was Caesar Augustus. He thought he was god and even demanded worship. When he commanded that a census be taken, I'm sure he thought that he and he alone was charting the course of history. But little did he know that God himself was reordering human circumstances to assure transport of his son Jesus from Nazareth to Bethlehem (Luke 2:4). People think they rule and reign. But they are just mere pawns in God's eternal plan and purpose.

Even during the time of the wicked reign of the Roman emperor Nero in the first century, Paul wrote to the believers in Rome, "Let everyone be subject to the governing authorities, for there is no authority except that which God has established. The authorities that exist have been established by God. Consequently, whoever rebels against the authority is rebelling against what God has instituted, and those who do so will bring judgment on themselves" (Romans 13:1–2). Paul understood that God was sovereign over Nero and was controlling all things and that God's people needed to submit to the rulers he had raised up.

I've often become emotionally drained and filled with worry over presidential elections. *Wouldn't that president destroy our country? God, you must give us so and so!* In those times, I felt like Habakkuk who complained to God about his circumstances. God responded by saying, "Look at the nations and watch—and be utterly amazed. For I am going to do something in your days that you would not believe, even if you were told. I am raising up the Babylonians, that ruthless and impetuous people, who sweep across the whole earth to seize dwellings not their own" (Habakkuk 1:5–6). Habakkuk couldn't imagine that God would consider using an ungodly nation to fulfill his purpose, so God had to teach him about his sovereignty. Habakkuk had to learn that God controls the nations and governments of the world.

And as I look back as elections have come and gone, I'm grateful for a loving God who is over all. Daniel 2:21 declares, "He changes times and seasons; he deposes kings and raises up others. He gives wisdom to the wise and knowledge to the discerning." Our times are in his hands and he does reign supreme. We can trust in him.

We can be assured that even when things seem like they are out of control, God knows what he's doing even in the tragedies of life (e.g., Holocaust, wars, earthquakes, Coronavirus, and so forth). We don't have to get uptight as if God's throne is vacant. He is actively involved, and this should give us confidence and hope.

Even the greatest tragedy that ever occurred on this earth was completely planned and purposed by almighty God. Jesus reminded the Roman guards who came to arrest him, "Do you think I cannot call on my Father, and he will at once put at my disposal more than twelve legions of angels? But how then would the Scriptures be fulfilled that say it must happen in this way?" (Matthew 26:53–54). The great evil that Satan had in mind was directed by God himself.

God controls all circumstances, even the moment all the powers of hell were centered on attacking and destroying God's Son. The good news is that God even used that event for his glory. If God can turn around the greatest tragedy in world history, can't he turn around our dark moments for our good and his glory? We also need to constantly remember God's tenderness and compassion for those who have experienced tragedies (e.g., those who been raped or whose loved one was murdered).

God works on a different level, and we don't fully comprehend his methods or his ways. But we can trust that he is good and loving. His ways are not our ways and his thoughts are not our thoughts

(Isaiah 55:8). His plan is always perfect and one step ahead of what we're thinking or planning. We can walk in victory as we believe that his plan and purpose will be accomplished.

The Pain and Triumph

By all standards, Laura Story was a success. According to *Christianity Today*, "She wrote the No. 1 worship hit "Indescribable" recorded in 2004 by Chris Tomlin, married a handsome athlete named Martin Elvington the next year, and began working in music and women's ministry at the 4,000-member Perimeter Church in Atlanta."[3] She won a Dove Award for Inspirational Album and two consecutive nominations for Female Vocalist of the Year. Incredible blessings by any standard.

But in 2006, her husband was hospitalized with a brain tumor and was kept alive through breathing machines. As a newlywed, she was faced with the very real fear of losing her husband. Surgeons were able to remove the tumor, but Martin continued to suffer from acute memory loss and significant vision problems. It was during that difficult time that Laura wrote the best-selling song *Blessings*. The song talks about how the blessings that God gives us are often disguised as painful trials.

Laura is far more fruitful today because of the trials and thorns she has experienced. She could not have written the runaway best-seller *Blessings* without the anvil of trials and difficulties. God perfectly planned those struggles to help her to trust him in a new way. He knows what he's doing and always has our best interests in mind.

The reality is that life throws us curve balls. It's not all rosy and sweet. Thorns often line our way. Jerry Bridges writes,

> God is in control, but in His control He allows us to experience pain. That pain is very real. We hurt, we suffer. But in the midst of our suffering we can rest in the knowledge that He is sovereign.[4]

Victory comes from knowing that God not only knows what we're going through but has planned those circumstances for our own good. John Calvin said, "Ignorance of providence is the greatest of all miseries, and the knowledge of it the highest happiness."[5] Calvin understood that God's grace and power are combined in his wonderful sovereignty. Notice how Calvin said that knowledge of God's sovereignty gives us the highest happiness. He does all things well.

God doesn't waste our mistakes—or our times of pain. He uses all things in our lives for his glory and our good. In fact, he has planned those pressure points and is perfectly controlling them. We will make mistakes—some big ones. The good news is that God is not condemning us. Rather, he is using those difficulties for our own good.

The best-selling book *Prayer of Jabez* dared believers to ask for God's prosperity and financial blessing. I do believe God prospers his people, but the problem with the word *prosperity* is that we often interpret it to refer to material possessions or riches in this life. But true prosperity involves spiritual riches, blessings that come from trials and sufferings in this life and rewards in the next life.

God can, and at times does, bless his children with wealth. Proverbs 10:22 says, "The blessing of the Lord brings wealth, without painful toil for it." God's blessings often come as a result of godly living and self-control. Believers prosper because they are not spending their money on wild living, and they understand the importance of saving for the future. In other words, they are exercising self-control, which is a fruit of the Spirit (Galatians 5:22–23). But there's also the reality that the prosperity of spiritual riches comes through pain, suffering, and weakness.

Most of us are quick to quote Romans 8: 28, but we forget verses 29 and 30, "For those God foreknew he also predestined to be conformed to the image of his Son, that he might be the firstborn among many brothers and sisters. And those he predestined, he also called; those he called, he also justified; those he justified, he also glorified." God often uses trials and difficulties to mold and shape us into the likeness of his Son, Jesus Christ. God's primary design is to make us like Jesus, not to provide personal happiness and certainly not to accumulate things and gadgets in this life. The victory, in other words, is to become more like Jesus, and God often uses painful circumstances to mold and shape us into Christ's image.

The movie *I Can Only Imagine* talks about Bart Millard's journey of writing the song *I Can Only Imagine,* one of the best-selling Christian songs of all time. Millard led his band, MercyMe, for many years but suffered from unforgiveness toward his abusive father. His bitterness plagued his singing, and it wasn't until he reconciled with his dad and helped care for him before his dad died that he really understood the grace of God. He then wrote the song *I Can Only Imagine* in ten minutes, and it has since catapulted him and his group to incredible success. God used an abusive situation to propel Millard to write a song that transformed millions.

In the book of Job, we see a man who was "The greatest man among all the people of the East" (Job 1:3). Yet, God's plan for Job was far greater than riches. God chose to test him. Would he trust God in the pain or turn away in bitterness? Job ultimately passed the test, and in the end, God doubled his prosperity (Job 42). An anonymous poet wrote:

When God wants to drill a man,
And thrill a man,
And skill a man
When God wants to mold a man
To play the noblest part;
When He yearns with all His heart
To create so great and bold a man
That all the world shall be amazed,
Watch His methods, watch His ways!

How He ruthlessly perfects
Whom He royally elects!
How He hammers him and hurts him,
And with mighty blows converts him
Into trial shapes of clay which
Only God understands;
While his tortured heart is crying
And he lifts beseeching hands!
How He bends but never breaks
When his good He undertakes;
How He uses whom He chooses,
And which every purpose fuses him;
By every act induces him
To try His splendor out—
God knows what He's about.

God knows what he's about, even though we do not. God is shaping us in all situations to accomplish a greater plan and goal. Wait for it. Watch for it. We struggle, worry, and doubt when all the while God has our best interests in mind.

Ruth has a book of the Bible written about her. She is a great example of God's sovereign plan and purpose through suffering. Naomi, Ruth's mother-in-law, lost her husband and two sons. Although Ruth's husband died and Naomi urged her to go back to her homeland of Moab. Ruth refused and followed Naomi back to Bethlehem in the land of Judah.

God's perfect plan was to prosper Naomi and Ruth in the land of Israel. In Bethlehem, God arranged the circumstances for Ruth to meet Boaz, a relative of Naomi, as well as a successful businessman. Ruth and Boaz eventually married, cared for Naomi, and gave birth to grandkids who ushered in the lineage of King David—the same family line of Jesus Christ (Luke 3:31). God was faithful to Ruth and he'll be faithful to us if we trust in him. Victory takes place when we trust his plan for our lives.

As a new missionary in Ecuador, I was placed on a pastoral team in which a successful businessman and co-founder of the church was leading the pastors. This man didn't like my steady stream of church growth suggestions. He viewed me as an idea person who wasn't ready to follow his plan. He asked my missionary supervisor, a veteran missionary on the field, to replace me with another missionary—one more willing to follow his agenda. I was crushed.

I pled with my missionary supervisor to give me a second chance. I felt like a failure, especially because this was my first four-year term of missionary service. And I felt it was unfair because I had not received any prior feedback from this business leader. Thankfully, they allowed me to stay on the team.

Weeks later, this same businessman casually mentioned in a team meeting that he'd like to strengthen the home group ministry in the church and wondered if someone on the team would like to take it over. I raised my hand, not only because I was passionate about small groups, but also to show my willingness to serve.

God did miraculous things through that home group ministry. The groups flourished from four to fifty. We were on the cutting edge of a ministry that helped the church grow from 550 to 950 in a short time. God used the struggle and the pain to launch me into my future ministry of small groups. Jesus was preparing me through the struggles and trials to lead the small group ministry that skyrocketed and eventually led to my life calling of studying, promoting, and writing about small group ministry.

God was planning this time throughout eternity, but to achieve the victory he had planned, he knew I needed pressure points to prepare me to receive his blessing. Yes, even in the trials and struggles, we can rejoice because victory is assured.

I encourage you to take time each day to meditate on all God has done in your life and how he is guiding and directing you. Write down what he reveals. Meditate on it. Rejoice in what God has done for you.

After God divided the Jordan River so his people could pass over on dry ground, he told Joshua to take twelve stones from the riverbed. These stones would help the Israelites to reflect on God's great work in future years.

You have those "stones of remembrance" in your own life, those times when God manifested his power and demonstrated his faithfulness. Reflect on them. As you remember how God has worked in the past, you can face the future with new confidence, knowing He's the same yesterday, today, and forever (Hebrews 13:8).

The Mystery

Kevin Strong and I went to Millikan High School together in Long Beach, California, and graduated in the same class. We reconnected in 1983 on the Long Beach City College speech team. Kevin was a communication teacher at a local community college and one of the speech team instructors. He had also recently become a Christ-follower. God used me to help Kevin grow in his faith, and God used Kevin to fine-tune my speaking skills. We became close friends in the process. He faithfully wrote letters to me during our time in Ecuador, and when we returned to California, Kevin was always available to get together and renew our friendship. Kevin had a gift of listening and always communicated transparently.

Around 1996, Kevin was diagnosed with brain cancer—a tumor in his spinal cord. Kevin tried everything to cure the cancer, including operations, new medicines, special foods, and healing prayer.

For many years, Kevin's plea was 'Take this away, Lord. Get rid of this." He was doubtful, anxious, and dissatisfied with God, wondering why this was happening to him. I took Kevin to a healing service in Pasadena and prayed for him often. But the tumor kept growing.

Then Kevin began to understand and trust God's sovereignty. He grew in his confidence of God, knowing that God was in control. Kevin still cried out to God and transparently shared his angst. Yet, he would come back to God's sovereign control, knowing that God could have healed him at any time.

Kevin died peacefully in October 2011. God chose to glorify his name through Kevin's life, witness, and trust. He's been with Jesus for some time now, rejoicing in perfect health and spiritual ecstasy. I envy him. Kevin's life was a testimony to God's grace and love. He was ready for eternity.

God often works in unexplainable ways. To remain in God's victory for our lives, we need to trust in him, even when we don't fully understand his purposes.

But what about evil, sin, and unrighteousness? Yes, God is over all. No wonder John Calvin declared, "All events whatsoever are governed by the secret counsel of God."[6] Scripture says that God is in control over darkness and disaster (Isaiah 45:7; Amos 3:6; Proverbs 16:4). Satan can't do anything without his permission (Job 1–2). Isaiah 45:7 says, "I form the light and create darkness, I bring prosperity and create disaster; I, the Lord, do all these things."

We need to realize that his ways are not our ways and his reasoning often doesn't coincide with our own. Mark R. Talbot writes,

> The mystery of why God has ordained the evils he has is as deep as the mystery of the evils in our hearts . . . It is not always our place to attempt to give an answer to those who are questioning God's goodness because of the evils that others have done to them or that they have done to themselves; sometimes we should just stand silently by their sides. Moreover, we will not always, right now, have these answers for ourselves. But in glory, the answer will be clear, when we see Jesus face to face. Then we will see that God has indeed done all that he pleased and has done it all perfectly, both for his glory and our good.[7]

Human logic can't fully comprehend God's sovereignty. It's a wonderful mystery. As believers, we can rest in God and his plan. He knows the way we take, and he does all things well.

On this side of heaven, we will not be able to fully understand how God's sovereignty relates to wars, starvation, abuse, untimely deaths, and so forth. Yes, sin and the curse are definite factors (Genesis 3). Free will is another. God is committed to allowing people to make choices, even if those choices are terrible and lead to very bad things happening. But God's encouragement to the believer is this, "Trust me; I'm in control." Something beautiful occurs when we can trust in a God who is bigger than the storm, the trial, and the difficulty.

Many great theologians in the past and present turn to the mystery of God when writing about God's sovereignty. The reality is that God's purposes are beyond our understanding. God knows all things and is in control, even when life appears so tragic and out of control. He has a perfect plan, but do we fully understand it? No. Do we have to understand it? No. William Cowper's hymn, "God Moves in a Mysterious Way," is as relevant now as it was in 1774,

> God moves in a mysterious way
> His wonders to perform;
> He plants His footsteps in the sea
> And rides upon the storm.
> Deep in unfathomable mines
> Of never failing skill
> He treasures up His bright designs
> And works His sov'reign will.
> Ye fearful saints, fresh courage take;
> The clouds ye so much dread
> Are big with mercy and shall break
> In blessings on your head.
> Judge not the Lord by feeble sense,
> But trust Him for His grace;
> Behind a frowning providence
> He hides a smiling face.
> His purposes will ripen fast,
> Unfolding every hour;

The bud may have a bitter taste,
But sweet will be the flow'r.
Blind unbelief is sure to err
And scan His work in vain;
God is His own interpreter,
And He will make it plain.

While speaking in Abuja, Nigeria a few years ago, I got an urgent message that my wife Celyce had severe stomach pain and was in the hospital. Celyce was diagnosed with diverticulitis which led to sepsis. She could have died, but thankfully, she was taken to the hospital before the poisons took over. My heart grieved but as I preached that morning from 1 Peter 4, my speaking took on new depths. I had to trust God.

As I rushed home from Africa, I clung to God's sovereignty, knowing that he was in control of all circumstances. Celyce did eventually improve after a colon operation. But the process was tumultuous for everyone involved.

As I visited Celyce in the hospital over the weeks, I saw people around her with far worse conditions—some who were dying or ready to die. I felt overwhelmed. How could I deal with the cries and hopelessness of those lying in those hospital beds? My only solace was to go back to God's sovereignty. I had to continually come back to God and his Word, trusting in his loving control. He is in control of all circumstances—absolutely everything. I can trust in my God, my rock. The victory came as I realized that God knows and is controlling all circumstances. Do I understand it? No. Do I believe it? Yes.

Life is difficult, but we can trust in him, knowing that he is guiding us and in control. He knows the way we take, and he will direct us. Paul said in 2 Corinthians 4:17–18, "For our light and momentary troubles are achieving for us an eternal glory that far outweighs them all. So we fix our eyes not on what is seen, but on what is unseen, since what is seen is temporary, but what is unseen is eternal." Here Paul is saying that the trials of this life are God's preparation for the next life. They still fit within the scheme of God's plan, but they are preparatory.

God will make it plain in his time. We can trust knowing that he takes the worst things that could happen and uses them for his glory. We don't have to fear life; rather, we can trust in the God who loves us. And the victory comes when we are securely resting in his promises.

I, like everyone else, can be glued to circumstances and terrified by future events. But when I come to God daily and place my life under his love and inerrant Word, I am renewed and more confident about what lies ahead. I'm encouraged that God has a perfect plan for my life and wants me to trust in him to guide me to the next step. This is true victory.

Don't Play God

God won't be bullied. He won't be cajoled and ordered to do things. We often want something so much that we begin to try to get God to do what we want, by the force of our will (or prayers). A lot of shenanigans have arisen to convince believers into thinking they simply have to claim a Scripture, a promise, or some other technique to get what they want. The opposite is true. We must submit to God's will and do what he wants.

Often Christians fail to receive answers they desire because questionable desires permeate their prayer requests. They are praying according to their own will instead of God's. James 4:3 says, "When you ask, you do not receive, because you ask with wrong motives, that you may spend what you get on your pleasures."

In 1978, for example, I applied for a bus driving job with the Los Angeles Unified School District. My primary reason for wanting the job was to make more money. I repeatedly "claimed the job by faith," declaring that it was "already mine." I attempted to deny all doubt and negative thinking, following the advice of a radio preacher.

There was only one problem: God didn't want me to have that job.

He had other plans for me. I missed the final driving test by one point (failure to leave the stick shift in gear when I parked the bus). Yet, it was a holy failure. Only a few months later, I left with Youth with a Mission for a short-term trip to Canada and remained in Canada for further studies. From there, God launched me into Christian ministry. As I look back, I now realize I had wrongly discerned the will of God.

Don't force your own will on God's. Don't "name it and claim it," thinking that God must respond as you desire. He is sovereign; you're not. Spending time in God's presence will help you discern God's specific leading. As you study the Word, meditate on his promises, worship in his presence, and listen to his voice, he will show you his specific plan for your life.

God has his timing. He will fulfill his will according to his plan. And we have the privilege of being part of that plan. He wants us to believe that he is sovereign and working out all things together for our good. He will do it. We must not push God. And when we simply trust his divine guidance, we cease from worry or fear.

Jesus does give us many promises about asking and receiving. He tells us that the Father wants to answer prayer (John 14–16). Yet, there's a huge difference between humbly asking and demanding. While God loves to bless his children, he's not our butler. We can't and shouldn't try to order God around. Instead, we are under his authority and his plan. God is working in us to fulfill his perfect plan and will.

At the end of the day, we must humbly submit to him and say, "Lord, if you will." Yes, we need to pray in faith believing, but ultimately, we can't demand God to answer our prayers. He knows our heart and often wants to give us the desire of our heart. But we need to allow him to mold us so that our desires become his desires.

In 1989, I was sure that God was going to open the door for me to be a professor at Fuller Theological Seminary and even fulfill Peter Wagner's mantle as the Donald McGavran chair of church growth. I pleaded with God and fully expected him to open the door. I claimed it over and over. But God didn't answer according to my will. He has his own purpose. God does whatever he pleases in heaven and on earth. I've had to learn this the hard way.

I've learned that whenever I begin to demand my way, God refuses to respond as I desire. At various times in my life, I've caught myself practically trying to convince God why he needed to act a certain way. In those same moments, I could have predicted that God would not answer my requests the way I wanted him to answer. He is God; I am not. I must humbly bow before him and confess my sin, giving him all the credit. As soon as I start feeling pressure like, "Lord, you better do this for me. You know I really want this," normally, it's a sign that God won't do it and my will is getting in the way.

The victory comes in waiting on God, in trusting in God, and ceasing to demand our will. God's will is better all the time. We can trust that God will do what he wants. As we do, the anxiety ceases.

Follow the Open Doors

Joan had been working part-time for Catholic Charities for many years. She loved her job and her family needed the extra income for expenses. Then her six-month-old started crying uncontrollably when she was gone and refused to feed on her stored breast milk while she was at work. John, her husband, had to take the child to Catholic Charities for a feeding, or Joan had to drive home. They didn't know what to do. Was it time to depend on John's salary?

Everything was super tight, but John was looking for additional work. He wanted her to stay home with their two small children, and she was open to it. Was this God's plan? Isaiah, her six-month-old, wouldn't stop crying, so they took it as a sign to quit the job at Catholic Charities. When they took this step, Isaiah stopped crying.

John was able to find extra work, and then landed an even better job. God's hand and prosperity were evident. Joan never regretted her decision to leave Catholic Charities. God continues to prosper them, and they rejoice in his clear direction.

The best advice I have for knowing God's plan is twofold: First, check God's leading with Scripture. God's leading will never contradict what he has already said in Scripture. So when discerning whether God is guiding us in a particular direction, we must first consult Scripture, submitting ourselves to God's inerrant Word.

Second, follow those doors that he is opening—those areas where he is blessing. What is he already doing? What doors are already opening? Those open doors are the ones for which we are uniquely equipped through gifts and talents. When God blesses and opens doors, it's because he has prepared us for that moment and he's glorifying himself through the situation. And it's through those doors that we experience the most victory and fruitfulness.

While God's Word gives general principles, we still need to exercise discernment about many details in our lives.

Take the Next Step

My daughter, Sarah, asked me one afternoon as we sat in a restaurant after a conference in Mexico, "How do I know God's plan right now?" She could see many things that she felt God wanted her to do, but she was concerned about fulfilling God's plan. I explained to her that God only asks us to take one step at a time. All we need to do is to take the next step.

We often feel overwhelmed because we think we must find and accomplish God's will all at once. But that's not the case. We simply need to take the next step right now, and then the next one will appear. The good news is that God is in us, both to will and do of his good purpose (Philippians 2:13). He has also ordered our steps, and we can be confident that the God who began a wonderful work in us will complete it until Jesus comes again (Philippians 1:6). He does have a perfect plan and purpose, and he's going to complete it.

He has our entire lives mapped out. We can just rest in his plan. It's like setting out for a journey with someone else driving who is completely trustworthy. You can sit in the front or back seat and just allow the driver to guide you. Unlike a human driver, God is perfect, and we can trust him 100 percent. We don't have to worry about anything (Matthew 6:25–26). As we trust in a loving God who is guiding each step along the way, we will grow in confidence and victory.

Points to Consider

- What is the main principle you've learned from this chapter? How will you apply it?

- Name some specific areas in which you have seen God sovereignly guiding your life?

- In what areas do you lack the faith that God is really in control?

- How will you rely on God's sovereignty to guide you in the future?

Spiritual Truth #2
Receive God's Grace

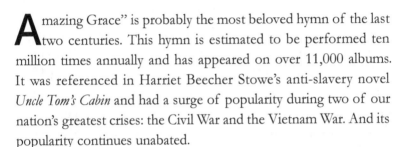

"Amazing Grace" is probably the most beloved hymn of the last two centuries. This hymn is estimated to be performed ten million times annually and has appeared on over 11,000 albums. It was referenced in Harriet Beecher Stowe's anti-slavery novel *Uncle Tom's Cabin* and had a surge of popularity during two of our nation's greatest crises: the Civil War and the Vietnam War. And its popularity continues unabated.

The author of "Amazing Grace," John Newton, was born in 1725 in London to a Puritan mother who died two weeks before his seventh birthday. She fervently prayed that her son would become a minister of the gospel, and God eventually answered her prayers. His father was a stern sea-captain who took John to sea at age eleven.

After many voyages with his father, Newton was forced to serve in the British navy. When he tried to desert, he received eight dozen lashes and was reduced to the rank of common seaman. He plunged into a depraved lifestyle and later said about those days, "I was exceedingly vile, little indeed if anything short of that animated description of an almost irrecoverable state described in 2 Peter 2:14, "Having eyes full of adultery, and that cannot cease from sin; beguiling unstable souls."[8]

Eventually, he became a slave trader, even owning his own vessel that transported thousands of slaves to England's far-flung empire. On a homeward voyage, while he was attempting to steer the ship through a violent storm, he experienced what he referred to later as his "great deliverance." He recorded in his journal that when all seemed lost and that the ship would surely sink, he exclaimed, "Lord, have mercy upon us." Later in his cabin, he reflected on what he had said and began to believe that God had addressed him through the storm and that God's grace had begun to work in him.[9] Newton took this as a sign from the Almighty and marked it as his conversion to Christianity.

God's grace transformed Newton. He renounced the slave trade and worked with William Wilberforce to abolish it altogether. He endeavored to see all men and women set free from both physical and spiritual bondage, writing to a fellow minister in 1764, "Remember your high calling, you are a minister and ambassador of Christ, you are entrusted . . . to carry the war into Satan's kingdom, to storm his strongholds and rescue his captives, you will have little leisure to think of anything else."[10]

In 1772, he wrote *Amazing Grace,* which expressed his gratitude for God's mercy and grace for saving him from a life of sin. On the wall of his study, he painted the text, "And thou shalt remember that thou wast a bondman in the land of Egypt, and the Lord thy God redeemed thee" (Deuteronomy 15:15).[11]

Amazing grace, how sweet the sound, that saved a wretch like me.

We Are Not Okay

Books such as *I'm Okay; You're Okay* are popular because people don't feel okay. The problem of guilt and condemnation is widespread. It's a way of life. An epidemic. People don't have solutions for their guilt. They feel condemned and unloved. Then they search for answers.

A person said to me recently, "This past year, I've felt waves of guilt and shame in my life." He went on to share about his mother who rejected him as a child. She moved out of the house when he was five and was replaced by a stepmother who never treated him as her own. He kept trying to overcome these feelings of guilt and shame by being a better person and through good works. He was trying to outweigh the bad by doing good things. This is a common but unfulfilling way that people deal with guilt and shame.

We need God's grace to live in victory. Only by faith in what Jesus did on the cross can we stand complete, and even perfect, before God.

It Is Finished

When Jesus died on the cross, he said these words, "It is finished." The price Jesus paid for man's sin was indeed finished on the cross. God provided the solution to guilt. He sacrificed himself on the cross (Philippians 2:5–11). Victory in Christ without the love and liberty that comes from the forgiveness Jesus paid for on the cross is impossible. God's grace replaces our heavy loads with his easy, light one.

It's not about what I have done but what Christ has done for me. I'm righteous in Jesus. He's my hope, my fullness, my all in all. In Jesus, I'm alive; I have peace. Jerry Bridges writes:

> We are all found to be in a state of ruin, but now God has provided a remedy: a righteousness that comes from God through faith in Jesus Christ. This righteousness is said to be "apart from law," that is, apart from any consideration of how well or not so well we have obeyed the law of God. . . . We are justified by His grace. It is because of God's grace we are declared righteous before Him. We are all guilty before God—condemned, vile, and helpless. . . . He owed us nothing; we owed Him everything. But, because of His grace, God did not consign us all to hell; instead, He provided a remedy for us through Jesus Christ.[12]

Those who know Jesus are completely clean and whole. All sin has been forgiven. Victory comes through Jesus and him alone. Scripture declares that there is now no condemnation (Romans 8:1) and that God loves us purely because of his mercy (Ephesians 2:4–5).

Our emotions go up and down. We feel good one moment and terrible the next. Even trying to become spiritual enough for God to use us can be deceptive. We won't always feel Spirit-filled and ready to serve, no matter how hard we try. Our feelings can deceive us.

Facts are much more reliable. And this is the fact: Jesus died in our place, the righteous for the unrighteous, the just for the unjust. Isaiah 53:5–6 says:

> But he was pierced for our transgressions, he was crushed for our iniquities; the punishment that brought us peace was on him, and by his wounds we are healed. We all, like sheep, have gone astray, each of us has turned to our own way; and the Lord has laid on him the iniquity of us all.

We are justified by our faith in Jesus and given a right standing before God. The easiest and quickest way to understand *grace* is the acronym:

G: God's
R: Riches
A: At
C: Christ's
E: Expense

We can receive all of God's riches because of what Jesus has done for us. Whenever we think we must add to what God has already done for us in Jesus Christ, we are unwittingly saying Christ's sacrifice was not enough. We start trusting in our own good works instead of his finished work. He has paid the price. God's Word says:

- "Therefore, since we have been justified through faith, we have peace with God through our Lord Jesus Christ, through whom we have gained access by faith into this grace in which we now stand" (Romans 5:1–2). Notice that we've been completely justified through faith in Christ and through Christ alone.

- "Since we have now been justified by his blood, how much more shall we be saved from God's wrath through him!" (Romans

5:9). We are completely justified and righteous because of God's grace. We are totally complete in him.

- "God made him who had no sin to be sin for us, so that in him we might become the righteousness of God" (2 Corinthians 5:21). The great exchange has taken place between us and God. He's taken our filthy rags and given us his own righteousness. We receive heaven instead of hell for one reason only: faith in Jesus Christ.

- Galatians 3:13 tells us "Christ redeemed us from the curse of the law by becoming a curse for us" [instead of us]. Jesus became a curse for us in order to redeem us from the curse of the law.

- "Blessed are those whose transgressions are forgiven, whose sins are covered. Blessed is the one whose sin the Lord will never count against them" (Romans 4:7–8). We are blessed because our sins have been cleansed and forgiven. No condemnation; only freedom because of what Jesus has done for us.

The entire Bible points to God's grace for his children through the cross of Christ. Even the Old Testament sacrificial system was fulfilled in Jesus. Good works were never enough. God sacrificed himself on our behalf. C. H. Spurgeon said:

> If you believe in Jesus, that is to say, if you trust Him, all the merits of Jesus are your merits, are imputed to you; all the sufferings of Jesus are your sufferings. Every one of His merits is imputed to you. You stand before God as if you were Christ because Christ stood before God as if He were you—He in your stead, you in His stead. Substitution! That is the word! Christ the Substitute for sinners—Christ standing for men and bearing the thunderbolts of the divine opposition to all sin, He "being made sin for us who knew no sin." Man standing in Christ's place, and receiving the sunlight of divine favor, instead of Christ.[13]

We can't merit God's favor. We simply believe God and trust in him. Without him, we can do nothing. In him, we can do all things. We are bought with a price—the price of Christ's blood (1 Corinthians 6:20). Scripture teaches that sin is so encased in who we are that good works won't get rid of it. It's like a cancer patient trying to get rid of the cancer by helping the poor. David says, "Surely I was sinful at birth, sinful from the time my mother conceived me (Psalm 51:5). Paul says, "For all have sinned and fall short of the glory of God" (Romans 3:23). Isaiah cuts through the deception of righteousness by good works when he says, "All of us have become like one who is unclean, and all our righteous acts are like filthy rags" (Isaiah 64:6).

I have a tradition of watching Mel Gibson's movie *The Passion of the Christ* on Good Friday each year. I then work my way through John Stott's excellent book *The Cross of Christ*. Stott writes, "God's people can yet overcome the devil 'by the blood of the Lamb,' and are assured that the final victory will be his and theirs, since the Lamb proves to be 'Lord of lords and King of kings.'"[14] The stories of Christ's death remind us that we are:

- justified
- forgiven
- reconciled
- cleansed
- set free
- released from bondage

The hymns ring true:
- "Nothing in my hand I bring; only to thy cross I cling."
- "Jesus paid it all; all to him I owe; sin had left a crimson stain, but he washed it white as snow."

It is finished. We don't have to earn God's favor. We are pleasing because of what Christ has done for us and our faith in Jesus.

Good works come as a result of trusting in Jesus—not the other way around.

You Are Loved. Right Now.

Martin Luther tried desperately to be good enough to receive God's love. After all, his own earthly parents were very demanding and hard to please. Luther recalled once, "[that] for the sake of stealing a nut, my mother once beat me until the blood flowed."[15] His father, Hans, also ruled his son with an iron fist. Luther said, "My father once whipped me so hard I ran away—I hated him until he finally managed to win me back."[16]

As a young monk, he tried to win his heavenly Father's favor by denying fleshly lusts and appetites. He would throw himself on the ground and grovel in the dust in his quest to deny the flesh. He thought he could beat himself into submission and that God would finally accept him. But his carnal desires kept coming back with a vengeance. He would then treat himself more severely. Things got worse. And all this was in the name of pleasing God and trying harder to live a holy life.

A wise overseer, Johann von Staupitz, saw Luther's frustration and recommended a change of venue. Johann sent him to study the Scriptures with the goal of teaching others. Luther had the opportunity to study the Bible in the original languages. What he learned, changed his life and the history of Christianity.

Luther understood the theme of grace and the authority of Scripture. He began to compare the traditions of the church with the Bible. In light of Scripture, the church was leading others astray and even teaching false doctrine. Luther recaptured the biblical truth that believers are justified through faith in Christ's death on the cross. He later wrote to a monk in distress,

> Learn to know Christ and Him crucified. Learn to sing to Him and say, 'Lord, Jesus, you are my righteousness, I am your sin. You took

on you what was mine; yet set on me what was yours. You became
what you were not, that I might become what I was not.'[17]

Luther became a new person as he walked by faith. He felt
new freedom and was able to preach with boldness. Even though
priests were forbidden to marry, Luther understood the freedom
he had through faith in Christ and married Katharina von Bora.
She became an intimate companion and helper in the ministry.

Grace changed everything. Luther's victory came from God's
grace and the fact that he was loved by God, not because of what
he had done or would ever do. Steve McVey says in his book,
Grace Walk,

> I did everything I believed a Christian should do to please God, and yet
> it was never enough. I could never experience joy in Jesus because of
> my focus on the spiritual disciplines still undone. No matter how many
> spiritual miles I traveled, I always saw 'ought to's' ahead of me stretch-
> ing into the horizon. I seldom enjoyed the scenery along the way.[18]

Sometimes, even the spiritual disciplines can become like laws
that condemn people. We must constantly remember that it's by
grace alone, and his grace then overflows into our lives and the
lives of others. Steve McVey goes on to say,

> It may sound strange, but I really began to enjoy the Bible when I
> realized that I didn't have to read it. From how much of the law has
> the Christian been set free? All of it! Is there a law that requires we
> read the Bible a certain amount of time each day? NO! Then why
> read it? Because we have a desire to fellowship with God in his Word.
> A grace-oriented approach to Bible study creates a hunger for it, while
> a law-oriented approach makes it a tiresome task that must be done.[19]

Satan loves to condemn us with those darts that say *never
enough*. Satan and his demons use a variation of this condemnation.
"You're not good enough." "You don't have what it takes." "You're
a failure." Scripture calls Satan the "accuser of our brothers and

sisters" (Revelation 12:10). He whispers in our ear that we haven't done enough or failed at what we tried to do for God. It's often in those silent, unprotected moments when our defenses are down and our minds are in neutral that Satan will come with doubts and dark thoughts.

When Satan throws his darts, we need to go back to Scripture again and again. We need to remember Romans 8:1, "There is now no condemnation." Only in the finished work of Jesus and his victory do we discover wholeness and freedom.

Our victory comes from God's undeserving love for us because of what Jesus has done on the cross. Isaiah says, "But he was pierced for our transgressions, he was crushed for our iniquities; the punishment that brought us peace was upon him" (Isaiah 53:5). We received the victory because of Christ's death. And God's love through Christ is inseparable. Paul, in Romans 8:34-39, proclaimed,

> Who then is the one who condemns? No one. Christ Jesus who died— more than that, who was raised to life—is at the right hand of God and is also interceding for us. Who shall separate us from the love of Christ? Shall trouble or hardship or persecution or famine or naked- ness or danger or sword? As it is written: "For your sake we face death all day long; we are considered as sheep to be slaughtered." No, in all these things we are more than conquerors through him who loved us. For I am convinced that neither death nor life, neither angels nor demons, neither the present nor the future, nor any powers, neither height nor depth, nor anything else in all creation, will be able to sep- arate us from the love of God that is in Christ Jesus our Lord.

We are victorious in Jesus. He accepts us because of his son Jesus. His life is our life. God's grace replaces the heavy load with an easy, light one (Matthew 11:30).

Learning to Lean

During the months of April and May 2016, my wife and I were invited to speak in ten different states in Brazil, flying in a small plane from state to state. I was able to handle the rigid schedule in the beginning, but as the days wore on, I became increasingly frustrated.

At the time, I felt that God's anointing on my speaking depended largely on my spiritual, mental, and physical preparation. In the beginning, I was able to find enough time for devotions, sleep, and preparation. But as the days progressed, our schedule made this impossible. We would arrive in a city late at night and be expected to meet in the hotel lobby very early. We loaded the van and were off to speak to the waiting crowds.

I came to a breaking point in Recife, Brazil. I was exhausted and my speaking suffered. I just fizzled out and lacked confidence in my morning talk. I asked Luiz, a fellow worker, to find a place where I could seek the Lord. I thought I could pick myself up through diligently praying and spending time with Jesus. My wife and I sat in that hot room as I tried to become more spiritual. My wife was relaxing but I was frustrated. People knocked on the door, trying to help us, but I was having "my devotions." But in reality, I was trying to become spiritual enough for God to use me. Yet, nothing worked.

My time came to speak in the afternoon, but I didn't feel ready. The speaker before me was dynamic, funny, and answered questions perfectly. He also was a native speaker. I dreaded speaking after him because I compared myself to him and felt inadequate. Suddenly, it was my turn. Even after all my extra devotions, I came across as dry, humorless, and stunted. As I looked out at the tired faces, I wondered if I should just stop. I longed to hide away somewhere. I cried out inwardly for strength but eventually wound down to a screeching halt. I asked the participants to break into groups and then after a short time, I fielded questions.

I didn't feel confident enough in my own spirituality to answer their questions, but the word *grace* popped into my mind. I desperately needed what I didn't possess. I needed something beyond my emotional, spiritual state. With God's grace in mind, I answered the questions boldly and grew in confidence as the questions continued. Grace sustained me. I then boldly prayed for people, signed books, took pictures, and everything ended well.

As we drove to the small plane to take us to the next Brazilian state, I reflected on what had happened. I realized that God's grace had sustained me and given me confidence—not my own good works and spirituality but rather, God's unmerited favor. I realized I would never have *enough* devotions, nor arrive at a place of spirituality to gain enough confidence. All I needed to do was rely on Christ's finished work and my standing in Jesus. Trusting in God's grace made me whole, gave me confidence, and prepared me for all situations, which allowed me to rest in Jesus.

God's grace gave me a new confidence in the weeks that followed. We still had many more conferences in various cities and states throughout Brazil. But as we flew or drove to the new locations, I had new hope and strength, which didn't depend on my preparation or skills but on Christ.

If we arrived at a city late, and I didn't get much rest or couldn't have a complete quiet time with Jesus, I remained confident in Christ's work in me. I leaned on God's grace—not my own—and he came through each time in a wonderful way. I felt strong, bold, and flexible. At various locations on that trip, I spoke to crowds of 3,000 or more and always had complete confidence. Why? I wasn't depending on my own spirituality or abilities, but in Jesus only. I realized that my confidence came from him and not myself. A new peace flooded my life and ministry.

I wrote this in my diary in May 2016, "Grace, grace, grace. It's all about grace. It's not about me. It's about you, and you are working in me. All things work together for good to those who love God. And I love God. Jesus, thanks. I can see why grace is such a powerful truth. I can just rest in God's work in me. I cease striving.

I cease from thinking about what I can do and what I can perform. My eyes are on Jesus and his work in me."

Meditate on God's Grace

So how do we live this grace walk? How does it play out? Walking in God's grace means that we go back to Scripture continually and remember all the promises of God about who we are in Christ. I challenge you to read each verse below and repeat the phrase in bold:

1. Romans 8:1 says, "Therefore, there is now no condemnation for those who are in Christ Jesus." **"I am no longer condemned."**

2. Romans 5:1 says, "Therefore, since we have been justified through faith, we have peace with God through our Lord Jesus Christ." **"I am justified by faith and have peace with God."**

3. 2 Corinthians 5:21 says, "God made him who had no sin to be sin for us, so that in him we might become the righteousness of God." **"I am righteous in Christ."**

4. Romans 6:18 says, "You have been set free from sin and have become slaves to righteousness." **"I am set free from sin."**

5. John 1:12 says, "Yet to all who received him [Jesus], to those who believed in his name, he gave the right to become children of God." **"I am a child of God."**

6. Romans 8:31–32 says, "What, then, shall we say in response to this? If God is for us, who can be against us? He who did not spare his own Son, but gave him up for us all—how will he not also, along with him, graciously give us all things?" **"God is on my side."**

7. Philippians 4:13: "I can do all this through him who gives me strength." **"I am in Christ and therefore I can do all things through Him."**

8. Ephesians 2:10 says: "For we are God's handiwork, created in Christ Jesus to do good works, which God prepared in advance for us to do." **"God has a perfect plan for my life."**

9. Ephesians 3:20 says, "Now to him who is able to do immeasurably more than all we ask or imagine, according to his power that is at work within us." **"God is capable of giving me far more than I could ever ask for."**

I also encourage people to read books on grace. There are many great ones out there:

- *Transforming Grace* by Jerry Bridges
- *Why Grace Changes Everything* by Chuck Smith
- *Grace Walk* by Steve McVey
- *Remember Who You Are* by Arron Chambers
- *TrueFaced* by Bill Thrall, Bruce McNicol, and John Lynch

Remind yourself through journaling about God's grace in your life. You'll soon find yourself walking in victory on a continual basis.

God's sovereignty leads to grace. When we believe that God is in control of all things, the next step is to understand that God loves us just as we are.

All of us have felt condemned. A thought, action, or lack of one. Condemnation can stalk and surround us. But we must remember that there is no condemnation. Like sovereignty, grace allows us to simply rest. I can trust in what Jesus has given me. He has done it. I'm righteous in him and in him only. I can find peace in Jesus.

A New Motivation to Serve

I consider Chuck Smith, founder of the Calvary Chapel movement, one of the most influential people in my life because his Bible teaching guided my early years of faith. I began attending Calvary

Chapel in 1973 and 1974. Even though I was radically changed by Jesus, I lacked direction. I needed Bible teaching.

More than any other theme, the topic of grace characterized Smith's life and ministry. His book *Why Grace Changes Everything* embodies this teaching. In the book, Smith talks about his years in ministry in which he was trying to be good enough to receive God's blessings. He writes,

> I was convinced some righteous plateau had to be reached before God would bless me. I believed that the moment I could achieve that high plateau, the Holy Spirit would fill me. And yet I was troubled by what I saw around me. How could people come off of the street and receive Jesus Christ as their Savior, stinking of booze and nicotine, and be baptized in the Holy Spirit right then and there? Yet they were. It wasn't fair. Here I had been walking with the Lord, serving Him all the way along, and they got blessed and I didn't. I couldn't understand the discrepancies of God. It was impossible for me to harmonize the teaching I had received with what I saw happening. If only I had understood God's grace![20]

After Chuck Smith understood grace, everything changed. He realized that God's blessing depended on what Jesus did for him on the cross—not his good works. Smith's message of grace gave hope to multitudes and the Calvary movement was born. Calvary Chapel welcomed hippies, drug addicts, and immoral people, trusting God's grace to transform them.

Beginning with the twenty-five person Costa Mesa congregation in 1965, Smith's influence now extends to more than 1,000 churches nationwide, some of which are among the largest churches in the United States, and hundreds more overseas. He has been called one of the most influential figures in modern American Christianity.

God's grace that leads to victory stirs us to serve God. Biblical grace teaches us good works are a result of God's love for us—not the other way around.

Paul's victory came as a result of knowing God's love. He said, "Even though I was once a blasphemer and a persecutor and a violent man, I was shown mercy because I acted in ignorance and unbelief. The grace of our Lord was poured out on me abundantly, along with the faith and love that are in Christ Jesus" (1 Timothy 1:13–14). And how did he respond to God's love and mercy? He said, "But by the grace of God I am what I am, and his grace to me was not without effect. No, I worked harder than all of them—yet not I, but the grace of God that was with me" (1 Corinthians 15:10).

The grace of God working through Paul stirred him to fully proclaim the gospel to the then known world (Romans 15:18–20). Paul accomplished a lot for Jesus, and many consider him the greatest church planter of all times. Yet, he wasn't doing these things to obtain God's favor, rather, he was compelled by Christ's love (2 Corinthians 5:14).

True Victory Is in the Cross

Before receiving Jesus Christ in 1973, I lived for my own desires and eventually, the emptiness landed me in despair. Nothing satisfied me. In my search for peace, I moved from oasis to oasis, but they were all mirages. Then I cried out to Jesus in my bedroom. He entered my life and gave me true peace. I was not good enough then and will never be good enough. Rather, the victory comes from his grace.

Through the cross of Christ, we are forgiven, loved, and cleansed from all sin. Hebrews 9:14 says, "How much more, then, will the blood of Christ, who through the eternal Spirit offered himself unblemished to God, cleanse our consciences from acts that lead to death, so that we may serve the living God!" Our victory will always lie in what Jesus has done for us.

All of history points to Jesus and the cross, all the way back from the garden through the sacrificial system through the prophets who predicted the Messiah to Christ's death on the cross. Now we look back and enjoy the fruit of what Jesus has already done for us on the cross.

The world calls this foolishness. How could God send his son to die on the cross for the sins of the world? But Scripture says God has chosen the weak things of this world to humble the strong and the foolish things to confound the wise (1 Corinthians 1:27-28). Why has he done this? So that we might boast only in God and his cross (1 Corinthians 2:1-5).

God sovereignly points all men and women to the cross where Jesus died. We can experience confidence when we rest on the finished work of Jesus. We are victorious because of what Jesus has done for us and who we are in him. It is finished. We are complete.

Points to Consider

- What is the main principle you've learned from this chapter? How will you apply it?
- Describe your journey of growing in God's grace.
- In what areas of your life are you depending on your own good works, rather than God's grace?
- What steps can you take to trust in God's grace daily?

Spend Daily Time with God

One day, a distraught man named Tim Corley nervously opened the door to my office. "I've tried everything," he blurted out. "I've been addicted to alcohol and drugs, and I've even tried a couple of religions. Now my wife wants to leave me. What can you do for me?"

Rarely had I witnessed such desperation in all my years of ministry. I had counseled many needy people, but Tim was different. He was clearly at the end of his rope. "I know that you've been sincerely searching for answers," I said, "but only Jesus Christ can fill the void in your heart." As I led him in prayer to receive Jesus Christ, the urgency in Tim's voice finally ended in relief.

God took control of Tim that day, and he became a new creation. A radiance and joy flooded his life. Before he departed, I counseled Tim to spend time with God daily.

At the new believers' class the next evening, Tim related how he had awoken early in the morning and spent time with his new friend, Jesus. Tim began a pattern of spending daily time alone with God that revolutionized his life and transformed him into a dynamic Christian. Over the years, as I watched Tim grow, I noticed the power of God in his ministry, in the renewal of his marriage, and in the prosperity of his work.

Tim still had his share of difficulties. Past marriage problems plagued him, and moving his restaurant to a new location required a heavy financial commitment. Yet, God's blessing followed him wherever he went. God was enlarging Tim's territory, and others noticed it.

I realized that the heavenly Father was blessing Tim as he spent time alone with him. The words of Christ were coming true before my eyes: "But when you pray, go into your room, close the door and pray to your Father, who is unseen. Then your Father, who sees what is done in secret, will reward you" (Matthew 6:6). Tim began to live in victory as he spent time with God, asking him for direction over every aspect of his life.

Going through the Motions

Recently, a pastor of a megachurch resigned, saying he was dry. He was busy doing the work of God without the life of God. He knew how to produce for God, but Jesus wasn't filling him daily.

Many believers try to do things for God each day without spending quality time with him. They race into daily life without allowing the life of God to pulsate through them. They know how to volunteer, lead a small group, or even preach, but they don't spend time with their Creator. They are busy but barren. Yet, the only lasting fruit comes from those things that God produces in us.

True victory—the kind that God honors—comes from spending daily time in his presence.

The Goal: Knowing God

The purpose of spending daily time with God is to develop an intimate relationship with God. It's about friendship rather than rules. The apostle Paul's yearning captures the heart of the quiet time: "I want to know Christ—yes, to know the power of his resurrection and participation in his sufferings, becoming like him in his death" (Philippians 3:10). Jeremiah covers similar ground in stating what the Lord says: "'Let not the wise boast of their wisdom or the strong boast of their strength or the rich boast of their riches, but let the one who boasts boast about this: that they have the understanding to know me, that I am the Lord, who exercises kindness, justice and righteousness on earth, for in these I delight,' declares the Lord" (Jeremiah 9:23, 24).

When you get together with a friend, do you list beforehand precisely what you are going to do and say? Of course not. You let the conversation ebb and flow—you just enjoy each other's company. That's how a quiet time with God should be, too. J.I. Packer said, "Knowing God is more than knowing about Him."[21] Packer goes on to describe the back and forth relationship that the believer has with God. It's not a one-way street. Yet, many Christians treat it as a ritual instead of a relationship.

During my own quiet time, I like to read the Bible, meditate on verses that stand out, worship, pray, and write in my journal. Some days, I'll spend more time in prayer, other days I'll linger in God's Word, and some days I'll journal more. My goal is to know God, not to follow a routine.

Don't allow your quiet time to become an evangelical rosary—the same mechanical prayers offered up day after day and week after week. The most important function of a quiet time is to allow you to break through into God's presence and come to know him more intimately. As soon as this goal of relationship with God becomes clouded with rules and rituals, we defeat our purpose.

Here's the story of a mother, in her own words, who went from having devotions to experiencing God:

> I'm not just reading my Bible or making requests anymore. I listen for Him, meditate on his Word. I write down what I hear Him saying to me. I try to make this time as honest, deep, and intimate as possible. When I started out doing quiet time, it was like I was getting my time card stamped by heaven—"Yep, she was here. A whole ten minutes!" Lately, I've had to drag myself away.[22]

This is the gist of what I'm saying. Quiet time is more than opening a Bible and saying prayers. It's experiencing the living God. It's communion with the King. It's finding him and then enjoying his blessed presence throughout the day.

Henry T. Blackaby, a Baptist preacher who wrote the best-selling book *Experiencing God*, says, "Knowing God does not come through a program, a study, or a method. Knowing God comes through a relationship with a person."[23] The quiet time is not a work to be performed but a relationship with the living God. The emphasis must remain on knowing him and growing in a relationship with God.

Don't become too focused on what you do in your quiet time; instead, focus on who God is. The best method for you will be the one that opens the door to experiencing the living God and draws you closer to him. The victory isn't in doing things for God but to know him and then to allow Christ to live through us.

God Desires to Spend Time with His Children

Did you know that God wants to spend time with you far more than you want to spend time with him? So often, we imagine that spending time with God is a job we must perform. To many, unfortunately, it's like lifting a heavy load to the throne of grace to please an angry God.

The Bible paints a different picture. We see a God who loves his children and longs to be with them. David said, "How precious to me are your thoughts, God! How vast is the sum of them! Were I to count them, they would outnumber the grains of sand—when I awake, I am still with you" (Psalm 139:17-18).

God is thinking about you all the time. Blackaby says, "God Himself pursues a love relationship with you. He is the One who takes the initiative to bring you into this kind of relationship. He created you for a love relationship with Himself. That is the very purpose of your lives."[24] God longs to spend time with you more than you can imagine. In fact, God desires to spend time with you so much that even now he's preparing your eternity, where you'll spend unbroken time with him (John 14:2).

Don't believe that God wants to enjoy you only when you are strong and capable. He understands exactly where you are right now. He enjoys you in your precise stage of development. Let God enjoy you. He chose you before the creation of the world and then called you to enter a love relationship with him. God desires to develop that love relationship with you. He desires to meet you in your daily quiet time.

Be assured that urgent needs will crowd your schedule and spoil your initiative to spend time with God unless you plan ahead—unless you make meeting with him the most vital appointment of your day. The words of Christ still ring true: "But seek first his kingdom and his righteousness, and all these things will be given to you as well" (Matthew 6:33).

Daily Bread

The combination of worship, powerful preaching, and intimate fellowship found in gathering with fellow believers deepens our relationship with Christ. But the impact is temporary; we need additional spiritual food to help us face our daily challenges.

When God provided bread from heaven (manna) for his people, the Israelites, he commanded them to gather daily only a day's amount. A day's worth of manna was fresh and good for only one day. We, too, need daily spiritual food to face the unique challenges that each day brings. Jesus said, "Each day has enough trouble of its own" (Matthew 6:34).

Yesterday's blessing and anointing won't prepare you to face today's cares, trials, and heartaches. You need fresh nourishment from Jesus today.

While God will use Sunday morning preaching to feed, transform, and encourage you, don't stop there. Spend time with him every day. As you daily feed on God's written Word, listen to his voice, and receive the filling of the Spirit, you will be renewed and encouraged to serve God more effectively.

And when we realize that our victory comes from God himself, we will gladly spend time with him to allow him to fulfill his purpose in us.

Meditating on God's Sovereign Grace

Vision leaks. So does trust. We can be strong and confident in God's plan one day and then doubt him the next. We can easily forget his promises and loving control over our lives. We start to worry and wonder how God is going to provide financially, resolve a relationship, or work in a loved one's heart. The devil loves to sow those seeds of doubt, sometimes during the waning moments of the night. We wonder how God can change difficult situations. We forget that God loves us, has a perfect plan for us, and will provide in all situations. We need to go back to his Word, his promises, our journal, and ask him to give us faith to believe.

I have found that a regular, consistent quiet time is the best remedy to resolve the doubts and fears and to restore trust in God's sovereign grace and power. Only he can set us free. Only he can set our heart and mind at peace and rest.

Each day when we spend time with God, we remember God's grace—who we are in Christ, and the fact that God is controlling all things. Our daily quiet time reminds us of his promises. We feed on his Word and get to know him better. Those who changed the course of history prioritized their time with God as the most important event in each day. LeRoy Eims said,

> People who have been used of God are those who have met with God on a daily basis. They have so ordered their lives that they have

found time to pray and read the Word of God. Quite often they do this in the early morning before work presses in, before the phone rings, and before the demands of the day are upon them.[25]

They realized that success in life required utter dependence on God. Below are a few examples of those who changed the course of history:

- Martin Luther declared, "I have so much business I cannot get on without spending three hours daily in prayer."[26]

- George Muller, the famous man of faith, not only developed his own personal quiet time, but he also asked all workers in his orphanage to spend an hour in prayer *during regular work hours*. Muller knew that he'd get far more out of his workers if they were spending time with the Master.

- John Montt, the leader of the modern missions movement in the twentieth century said, "After receiving Jesus Christ as Savior and Lord and claiming by faith the fullness of the Spirit of God, I don't know of any other discipline that produces more spiritual blessing than spending daily quiet time of at least one-half hour with the living God."[27]

- A. B. Simpson, founder of the Christian and Missionary Alliance, said, "I'm nothing without spending time alone with God."[28]

- David Yonggi Cho, pastor of the largest church in the history of Christianity, awakes every morning to commune with the living God. He believes that the reason his church has grown so large is a result of his quiet time.

- Bruce Wilkinson, author of *The Prayer of Jabez*, made a commitment to get up each day at 5:00 a.m. to read the Bible, journal, and to pray and seek God until he found him.[29] God transformed his life and ministry.

The writer of Hebrews describes running the race in the light of those who have run before us: "Therefore, since we are surrounded by such a great cloud of witnesses, let us throw off everything that hinders and the sin that so easily entangles. And let us run with perseverance the race marked out for us" (Hebrews 12:1).

Spending time in God's presence sharpens our understanding of God's sovereignty and grace and allows us to know God in a deeper way. Quiet time flows from God's grace because an important part of spending time with God is understanding his riches and believing that God is sovereignly guiding us. The goal of our quiet time is to know God, which involves disciplines like reading Scripture, meditating on God's Word, worship, listening, intercession, and journaling.

I'm not a passive writer on the topic of quiet time. I didn't always believe in the importance of making my quiet time a daily activity. At times I'd say, "I'm too busy today, God. I'll do extra devotions tomorrow." I didn't realize how much I would need fresh nourishment today—as well as tomorrow.

Without my time with God, I flounder through my day without the Spirit's control to face life's difficulties. I need God's victory in my life that comes from spending time with him and his staying with me throughout the day.

My quiet time provides me with a chance for a daily checkup—a time to express my cares and concerns of each new day. During my quiet time, I meditate on God's plan and purpose for my life, family, and ministry. I can talk directly to the God who loves me, who chose me before the creation of the universe, and who is as close as the air I breathe. I become excited as I understand who he is and how he is working in my life. I meditate on what he has done and what he's going to do.

Meditating on the sovereignty of God opens our eyes to see where God is already working so we can follow his leading. This knowledge gives us confidence and hope for the future.

I've Tried, but . . .

For many, quiet time is not an exciting adventure in which they get to know God; rather, it's a lot like eating liver, attending a required board meeting, or taking out the trash. "I'll do it by the sheer force of my will—nothing more." A friend of mine once said:

> Dryness has been my problem in the past . . . no heartfelt time with the Lord, but instead just going through the motions. I fulfilled my quiet time out of duty . . . because I thought it was the right thing to do. I wanted to get something from God. Now I want to be with him, communicating with him, "touching" my Father.

At one time or another, we have all felt dryness when spending time with God. If you are struggling with spending regular time with God, you don't need guilt heaped on you. What you do need is concrete solutions to make your quiet time fresh.

Perhaps someone has tried to tell you that you're not really a Christian unless you have a quiet time. If so, rather than being a delight, spending time with God could become a burden.

My advice is to ask God for the desire to spend time with him. Paul says, "But the fruit of the Spirit is love, joy, peace, forbearance, kindness, goodness, faithfulness, gentleness and self-control. gentleness and self-control. Against such things there is no law" (Galatians 5:22). Self-control is the fruit of the Spirit of God. As we ask Jesus to fill us, he'll give us the self-control to pray, to spend time with him daily, and to even desire that special time.

My good friend Kevin Strong, who is now in heaven, said to me, "Joel, many people know they should have a quiet time, but they don't have a desire to spend time with him. You need to write about how to have a desire for daily devotions."

"Kevin, only God can give a desire," I responded. "I can't give people a desire. Only God can do this." As we ask him for a desire, and he fills us with the Spirit, the resulting fruit of self-control will stir believers to spend daily time with him.

Is It Enough to Pray "On the Hoof"?

The Bible tells us to pray continually (1 Thessalonians 5:17) and to live by the Spirit (Galatians 5:25). Scripture also invites us to spend specific time with God (Matthew 6:5–6). Does one replace the other? Some people think so. You hear this in their reply, "I pray all the time. I don't need to spend specific time with God." Or, "I have my quiet time in the car on the way to work." Having a quiet time on the way to work, especially on a big city freeway is not quiet or focused. Both personal time with God as well as praying continually are essential.

Personal time with God refreshes and empowers us to walk in the Spirit for the rest of the day. After spending time with God, you will notice a new attentiveness to his presence in your daily activities. Having a quiet time stimulates the believer to then pray continually throughout the day.

Consider your relationship with your spouse. Kissing him or her on the cheek is an important thing to do intermittently throughout the day, but to keep the fire burning, you'll need to find time for more than that—like a passionate embrace or a special romantic time.

Still, filling up during your quiet time doesn't deny the need to pray continually throughout the day. Frank Laubach, author of many books on prayer, literacy, and justice, says, "A devotional hour is no substitute for 'constantly abiding,' but it is an indispensable help; it starts the day right. But the day must keep right. We should cultivate the habit of turning to God whenever we stop any piece of work and look around to ask what to do next."[30]

So both are important. One feeds on the other. Praying continually is the afterglow of receiving God's fullness in our quiet time. Just don't make the mistake of substituting one for the other.

Quiet Time Versus Continually Abiding

Quiet Time	Continually Abiding
• Receiving God's fullness	• Maintaining God's fullness
• Studying God's Word	• Remembering God's Word
• Waiting on God	• Walking with God
• Praying about particular matters	• Praying moment by moment

Getting to Know God through His Word

Begin your quiet time by reading the Word of God. The Bible is God's love letter to us, instructing us on how to live a holy, successful life. It will not only keep you from sin, but it will reveal who God is. You will begin to understand his nature, how much he loves you, and his perfect plan for your life. With God's Word filling your heart, you will be able to naturally flow into worship, confession of sin, listening to his voice, and praying for others.

You can find many great devotional guides on the market today. My only caution is that you don't allow any book or guide to replace God's holy Word. All tools are only faint mirrors of the Bible.

The Bible is without error. This is not true of other books or guides. We can read the Bible with full confidence, knowing that everything we read in it can be fully trusted (2 Timothy 3:16). As you open God's Word in your quiet time, you can be assured that God himself is talking to you.

Not only is God's Word inspired, but we also have a divine helper to aid our understanding when reading it. Jesus promised that the Holy Spirit would guide us into all truth (John 16:13). Since the Holy Spirit lives within every born-again believer, he will be right there to reveal God's truth to you. As the apostle Paul said, "What we have received is not the spirit of the world, but the Spirit who is from God, so that we may understand what God has freely given us" (1 Corinthians 2:12).

Before reading the Bible, ask God for his wisdom. You might say, "Holy Spirit, help me understand the Bible and apply it to my daily life." This is the prayer that God loves to hear and answer.

God has also given us the promise of success and prosperity when reading his Word. This is not true of any other book or guide. Referring to the one who reads and meditates on God's Word, Psalm 1:3 says, "Whatever they do prospers." In Joshua 1:8, God pronounces prosperity and success to the one who meditates on and obeys his Word. These are just a few of the many Bible promises to those who delight in God's Word. The real question is this: Can we afford *not* to read his Word daily?

When you commit to spending time with the God who ordered the stars, the universe, and the pregnant mother's womb, he will order your day and bless you. He will show you how to reschedule or delete an unnecessary activity to get more quality time out of your day. God illuminates our minds as we meditate on him.

Victory starts with God. He is the only one who can grant that victory. As you spend time with the one who created all things, he'll give you wisdom and guidance. He'll also prosper all you do.

Worship First; Service Second

The divine order of action as given in the Bible is worship first; service second. Jesus said, "Worship the Lord your God, and serve him only" (Matthew 4:10). This order is repeated later when Jesus says, "Love the Lord your God with all your heart and with all your soul and with all your mind." Afterward, comes the second command, "Love your neighbor as yourself." (Matthew 22:37, 39).

How do you worship God in your quiet time? You might sing a hymn or favorite worship chorus, wait in silence, or read a Psalm. I normally read God's Word first and naturally follow by worshiping God. Paul Cedar once said,

My words of praise and worship often flow from my times of Bible reading and meditation. Then I express to Him some words of praise and worship from one of the psalms or another passage of Scripture. Sometimes a certain song or hymn of praise will come to mind when I am meditating on my Bible reading or when I am reading one of the psalms as an expression of praise and worship to God. Otherwise, I proceed sequentially through my hymns and praise songs.[31]

By worshipping God in our daily quiet time, we're saying, "Lord, my service and work are not nearly as important as you are. Lord, I place you first in my life. I want you more than anything else."

An important part of worship is being still. The psalmist said, "Be still, and know that I am God" (Psalm 46:10). I like the late Eugene Peterson's radical and refreshing translation of this passage in *The Message*, "Step out of the traffic! Take a long, loving look at me, your High God, above politics, above everything."

God can speak anytime, anywhere, and anyplace. He's not bound to speak in a temple or in any physical place. God's new temple is our bodies, and the Holy Spirit dwells there all the time. The most common time, however, for God to speak is when his children are spending quality time in his presence. During our quiet time, God has our attention. We've dedicated this time to him. Our heart is prepared through the Word, worship, and confession. The static is gone. The signal comes in loud and clear. We're tuned into the right station.

After a full day of calling down fire, seeing false prophets killed, and seeing miracles, the prophet Elijah was drained. He needed rest, yet, he still had to worry about Jezebel's vow to kill him. At this point, Elijah's spirituality left him, and he did something very natural—he ran for his life. God was gracious to Elijah and provided him with food and rest. Later, God spoke to Elijah, saying:

"Go out and stand on the mountain in the presence of the LORD, for the LORD is about to pass by." Then a great and powerful wind tore the mountains apart and shattered the rocks before the LORD, but the LORD was not in the wind. After the wind there was an earthquake, but the LORD was not in the earthquake. After the earthquake came a fire, but the LORD was not in the fire. And after the fire came a gentle whisper. When Elijah heard it, he pulled his cloak over his face and went out and stood at the mouth of the cave. Then a voice said to him, "What are you doing here, Elijah?" (1 Kings 19:11–13).

We all like the sensational prophetic word that tells us exactly what to do—the letter in the mail with the $100 bill, the phone call at the exact moment of need. Yet, here God didn't reveal himself through an earthquake, a fire, or a mighty wind. He chose to come to Elijah in a still, small voice.

Do you want victory in your personal life? Spend time with God. He will give you that victory. You'll be filled with new passion and strength as you meet those challenges around you. He'll show you the next step.

Confession of Sin

In biblical times, dirt roads were the norm. Since everyone wore sandals, no matter how hard a person tried to keep his or her feet clean, they would naturally pick up the dirt and dust of the Roman roads. Foot washing wasn't a religious rite; it was a practical need.

Quiet time is our foot washing. It's the time to come to God and his Word, asking him for cleansing, restoration and renovation. The apostle John said, "If we confess our sins, he is faithful and just and will forgive us our sins and purify us from all unrighteousness" (1 John 1:9).

The good news is we can find cleansing and healing in the blood of Jesus Christ. Hebrews 9:14 says, "How much more, then, will the blood of Christ, who through the eternal Spirit offered himself unblemished to God, cleanse our consciences from acts that lead to death, so that we may serve the living God!"

Jesus desires to work within us as we recognize our sin, confess it, and receive his cleansing. Jesus is able to set us free from Satan's bondage. He's able to give us the victory we need. When we know we are forgiven and cleansed, we can behave confidently in whatever we do and say.

Even as mature Christians, we unconsciously pick up bad habits, wrong thoughts, and succumb to Satan's darts. The world, the flesh, and the devil lurk in the least expected places. You can hardly watch TV, browse the internet, listen to the radio, drive down the freeway, or overhear a conversation without seeing wicked images, worldly overtures, or outright sinful behavior.

The good news is that there is power in the blood of Jesus Christ to cleanse us from all sins. Quiet time provides the perfect opportunity to let God speak to us, restore us, renew us, and give us the power to overcome the enemy. God invites us to be cleansed daily and renewed to live victoriously.

The Power of Prayer

The dictionary defines prayer first, as an act of communion with God and second, as reverent petition made to God.[32] Prayer is an intimate dialogue between Father and child. Petition, while important, is a result of our communion with him.

Many people believe that prayer and daily quiet time are the same thing. You can detect this when asking about their quiet time. "Sure, I pray," is often their quick response. Yet, prayer is just one aspect of quiet time.

George Muller, a man who modeled effective prayer, wrote, "When we pray, we speak to God. This exercise of the soul can be best performed after the inner man has been nourished by meditation on the Word of God."[33]

In my own quiet time, I like to receive spiritual strength from the Word and worship before prayer. As I find strength through

God's Word, I'm more encouraged to commune with God and pray for others.

The Word of God tells us about God's willingness to answer. This principle is captured in Christ's reply to the leper who questioned his willingness to heal. We read, "He reached out his hand and touched the man. 'I am willing,' he said. 'Be clean!'" (Mark 1:41).

God invites us to ask for a renewed filling of the Holy Spirit. Jesus said, "If you then, though you are evil, know how to give good gifts to your children, how much more will your Father in heaven give the Holy Spirit to those who ask him!" (Luke 11:13). Jesus is telling us that the heavenly Father desires to pour out his Spirit on us. All we need to do is ask. And we need his filling to experience victory in all we do and say. Don't hesitate to ask Jesus for his filling. He longs to give you the strength you need as you become God's instrument for those you meet.

God could fill us on a crowded bus, at the breakfast table with chattering kids, in a classroom, or wherever we happen to be. Most of the time, however, he chooses to fill us when we've meditated on his Word, sought him, and confessed our sin. As a result of spending time with him, we're refreshed and renewed to face the dry desert around us.

Journaling

Journaling is writing down our thoughts, illuminations from God, applications of biblical truth, praise reports, accounts of struggles, and whatever else we believe is important to write down.

Many have heard or read *Anne Frank: The Diary of a Young Girl,* the famous diary of a Jewish girl hidden for two years with her family during the Nazi occupation of the Netherlands. Anne wrote about her diary, "I can shake off everything as I write; my sorrows disappear, my courage is reborn."[34]

Quiet time is the perfect time for such journaling—to write down the latest disappointment, promotion, conflict, or victory. Journaling is helpful for a number of reasons:

1. **To find comfort in times of trial.** When everything is rosy and normal, I don't feel the need to write. But during times of conflict or defeat, or when I'm on the ground looking up, my diary offers comfort. I've had to keep this fact in mind when reviewing my diary from the past year. I'm more prone to write about a disagreement with my wife than the many peaceful evenings I've spent with her. Why? Because the conflict was a more intense time when I felt the need to call out to God and find his wisdom. The clarifying balm of my journal helped me overcome the problem.

2. **To clarify our thinking.** Writing down our thoughts helps us to see things from more than one perspective. Vague impressions or unclear thoughts begin to untangle themselves as we write them down. In some cases, we realize we have knowledge we didn't know we possessed.

3. **To reflect on what God has done in our lives.** During my quiet time, I will occasionally open my journal and look at pages of past entries. As I'm reading, I will remember the past situation—the conflict, the victory, or the longing. I often find myself thinking, "Wow, time has passed so quickly. I'm so grateful for God's work in my life. He's never let me down."

As you practice writing down thoughts in your journal on a regular basis, your writing will soon become a refuge. You'll find yourself writing during times of pain, difficulty, confusion, or joy. Over time, this written record will become a source of encouragement as the promises of God are verified or as your struggles finally end. You'll love to look back at what God has accomplished in your life.

You'll rediscover that God himself was guiding you and that he was faithful to take you through the difficult challenge. You'll be encouraged to trust God for the next bend along the road, knowing that he'll be faithful once again, just like he always has.

Set the Amount of Time

My recommendation for those who are just starting their quiet time is to spend half an hour each day, with the goal of graduating to one hour. "Why even set a specific time?" you might ask. "Why not spend as much time as necessary?"

Because when you first spend time with God, it will be hard to feel his presence. You'll probably feel dry and wonder why you even needed to practice such a ritualistic exercise. It takes time to develop intimacy with God.

In those early days, expect to press ahead, even if you receive little during your quiet time. Mike Bickle, a Kansas City pastor who is well-known for his twenty-four-hour prayer ministry, writes:

> When you first spend 60 minutes in a prayer time do not be surprised if you come out of it with only 5 minutes you consider quality time. Keep it up, and those 5 minutes will become 15, then 30, then more. The ideal, of course, is to end up with both quantity and quality, not one or the other.[35]

C. Peter Wagner writes, "It is more advisable to start with quantity than quality in daily prayer time. First, program time. The quality will usually follow."[36]

As you set the amount of time and persist, you'll develop more quality as time goes on. You will grow in your delight to spend time with God the more you do it. Hunger produces more hunger.

When I began dating my wife, our initial time together was awkward. We weren't sure what to say, how to act, or what to expect. As we spent more time together, our relationship became more natural. We understood each other better, and we could enjoy each other more fully. As you consistently spend time with God, you'll notice a new freedom in his presence. The quantity of time will become more qualitative as you grow in your relationship with him.

You'll find yourself missing spending time with God when you don't have it. You'll long to linger in his presence, receiving his victory as you face your challenges each day.

Make It a Habit

A habit is a routine behavior that is repeated regularly and tends to occur subconsciously. Make your daily quiet time a habit. Allow it to become part of your routine so when you don't have it, you'll miss it. Don't wait for the urge. Make it a discipline, and the urge will come. When you blow it and can't spend time with God, don't let the devil condemn you. Remember the priority of grace. You will fail. Circumstances will arise when it will be very difficult to keep your normal schedule. Take those exceptions in stride and don't give up.

The lack of consistency is one of the greatest hindrances to regular, daily quiet time. When asked how often they have a quiet time, people often respond, "When I feel like it." Many decide to spend their time with God when they get the urge. The underlying thinking is that it's more spiritual to spend time with God when you feel burdened. But while it's great to feel the burden and passion of God, that won't always be the case. More likely, you'll feel tired, busy, and preoccupied with other things.

It's best to develop the habit of meeting with God at the same time each day. The main reason is a pragmatic one: the likelihood that you'll have a quiet time will increase because you'll grow accustomed to setting aside that time period. You'll find yourself planning your daily activity *around* your quiet time, rather than trying to fit it into a crowded schedule.

When you do choose a time, share your choice with another person (spouse, roommate, parent, friend) and ask that person to pray for you. Having a person who will encourage you and keep you accountable can be a great help in keeping your commitment to a daily quiet time. And be sure to volunteer to do the same for someone else.

Someone has said that a journey of a thousand miles begins with a single step. Take that first step now. After a while, spending daily time with God will become a habit. Yes, there are times you will fail but ask him to fill you and give you self-control (Galatians 5:22–23).

God's Reward

I had the opportunity to better understand the relationship between quiet time and God's blessing. For my doctoral dissertation, I polled 700 lay leaders in a wide variety of churches to determine why some leaders were more fruitful than others. I was surprised to discover that a leader's success had nothing to do with personality, social status, education, or spiritual gifting. But it had everything to do with the amount of time they spent with God. This consistently appeared as the most important factor in my study.

I wasn't expecting this correlation. I thought I'd discover more natural, human reasons for success in ministry. Yet, the correlation is a logical one. During quiet time with the living God, we hear God's voice and receive his wisdom and direction. It stands to reason then, that Spirit-filled lay leaders, moving under God's guidance, will have an untouchable sense of direction and leadership. God grants them success.

God desires to reward you and make you more effective in your job, with your family, in your studies, and in your interpersonal relationships. He wants you to walk in victory and confidence. The quiet time is that place in which the Father sees and will reward you openly. Remember Christ's promise, "But when you pray, go into your room, close the door and pray to your Father, who is unseen. Then your Father, who sees what is done in secret, will reward you" (Matthew 6:6). You'll discover new victory in all you do and say because of his unseen presence.

Of course, the best reward of all is fellowship with the living God and getting to know him better. This should be our most important target and chief goal. The more time we spend with God, the more we get to know him and become like him (1 John 3:1).

Points to Consider

- What is the main principle you've learned from this chapter? How will you apply it?
- On a scale of 1–10, how consistent is your quiet time?
- What can you do to improve your quiet time?
- Describe your daily Bible reading plan in your quiet time?

Invest in Your Intimate Circle

I saw a television program in which a high-profile husband and wife pastoral/preaching team told their church on live TV that they were getting a divorce, but that they would continue ministering as usual. He would continue pastoring the church, but she would move to another state to lead her already established parachurch ministry.

They are acting as if nothing happened. Have we descended into such an abyss that our Christianity does not work at the most intimate levels of our lives?

I can imagine that some in the congregation felt justification when they heard the news that morning. After all, those listening were just as likely to have experienced a divorce as the unchurched population. Mark Galli writes,

> . . . the rate at which evangelicals divorce is hard to distinguish from the larger culture's, and the list of reasons for divorce seems no different: "'We grew apart.'" "'We no longer met each other's needs.'" "'Irreconcilable differences.'" The language of divorce is usually about the lack of self-fulfillment.[37]

One of the saddest things about Western culture is the breakdown between the personal and public lives of people. It has become acceptable to say, "I don't care what he or she does in private. That's none of my business."

God cares. And he cares enough to intervene. He's not out to get us. Rather, he wants to mold and shape us to become like himself. He wants to bring us into his image, so that we will be like him and that we will learn to love and enjoy him all the days of our lives.

Famous author and speaker, John Maxwell, has been married to his wife, Margaret, for over forty years. Maxwell writes,

> I'm still married to the love of my life, both my kids are married with children (my grand angels!), and we all still enjoy spending time together. Wrapping my definition of success around those I love the most made the difference. And really, when you reach the end of your life, what will be most important to you? Dusty awards granted by acquaintances, or deep connection with those you love? [38]

When Maxwell was thirty-nine years old, he noticed that many of his college friends were getting divorced. He and Margaret didn't think they were in danger, but they knew that many of their friends had also thought their relationships were indestructible. John's career was taking off, and he didn't want to lose his family in the process. That prompted him to make one of the key decisions of his life, rewriting his definition of success. Instead of acclaim, advancement, or achievement, he decided that for him:

Success means having those closest to me love and respect me the most.

This made success for him possible only if he included his wife and children in the journey. From that moment on, his success depended on putting family first.

He writes, "If you want to truly succeed in this life, you need to ask yourself a question: Is your pursuit of success drawing you closer to—or farther from—the most important people in your life?"[39]

When I heard Maxwell utter these words at a Promise Keepers rally in July 1996, I didn't catch the full weight of what he said that afternoon, but over the years, I've had time to reflect on life, ministry, and relationships. Maxwell's words have convicted me to prioritize what really matters. Even though community involves many areas of our lives, the most important community relationships are those closest to us. If community doesn't work there, it really doesn't work.

God's victory comes through success in our relationships. The Christian life needs to be worked out with those closest to us. The result is victory.

Relationships Do Matter

People do not think their personal relationships define success. They think that their outward success or personality is what matters the most.

Many Christian couples live under the same roof but are completely separated emotionally and have never been able to reconcile. They only communicate enough to manage finances and other administrative tasks.

One of my childhood friends, John, was so full of life and fun. Now he lives a hermit existence with his mother and only occasionally comes out of the house to move the car or do other essential functions. Maybe he's just afraid. His mother, who rarely leaves the house, was probably hurt deeply when her second husband committed suicide. God desires to transform John and his mother. They need God's love to break through the pain and then lead them to loving relationships with others.

True victory is having success with those who are closest to us and allowing Jesus to mold and shape us through those intimate relationships.

Prioritizing Intimate Relationships

I have the privilege of speaking to crowds around the world. The people I meet at those events don't know me personally. Perhaps they've read one of my books, and hopefully, I've given them a good impression while speaking. Yet, they don't know the real me. And I don't know them.

The crowd doesn't know us personally. We can hide from the crowd. We can say just enough to make us look "real" but too little to be truly vulnerable.

My wife and family, however, know me intimately. They see Joel Comiskey close up and know how successfully my faith translates into the nitty-gritty of life. They witness how I deal with real-life circumstances and whether I'm living the Christian life, rather than just talking about it. Words take a backseat to action and lifestyle. They know how I act and who I am.

I have failed at times and sinned. But how did I rebound? How did I recalibrate? God's work of grace starts with the inner circle. In that circle, we receive criticism, true encouragement, and make mid-course corrections. As we pass the inner circle test, God can then use us in greater spheres of influence.

God's not interested in public success without private victory. The two are inseparable. In fact, Christ prioritized teaching twelve disciples for three years so they might later pass the multitude test. He wanted those few to successfully apply his words in daily life and action. By concentrating on them, Jesus would eventually reach more and more people. But he needed to focus on quality first. The quality would bring the quantity.

Christ's intentional concentration on the twelve gains significance by knowing that the multitudes wanted to take him by force and crown him King (John 6:15). Even the Pharisees admitted that the world had gone after him (John 12:19). But Jesus focused on the ones who would minister to the masses. They would change the world, and Jesus focused on them first. They were his priority.

This is what God calls us to do today. He wants us to focus on those closest to us. Those are the ones who need us most. Christ is also concerned about relational success with those we are closest to—the ones who know us best. The Apostle Paul also supported this relational principle in his ministry as he admonishes us in Galatians 6:9,10, "Let us not become weary in doing good, for at the proper time we will reap a harvest if we do not give up. Therefore, as we have opportunity, let us do good to all people, especially to those who belong to the family of believers".

Who are those closest to you? Only you can answer that question, depending on your circumstances. If you're married, I believe your spouse is number one on your list. If you're a child, it's your parents, brothers, sisters, and friends. If you're divorced and have children, those closest to you would be your children. If you're single, perhaps your inner circle would be close friends or believers you meet with regularly.

God's Intimate Circle

You won't find the word "Trinity" in the Bible. Scripture is abundantly clear, however, that there is only one God and that all three persons (Father, Son, and Holy Spirit) are called God. The Bible teaches that:

- The Father is God: "yet for us there is but one God, the Father, from whom all things came and for whom we live" (1 Corinthians 8:6)

- Jesus is God: "But about the Son he says, 'Your throne, O God, will last for ever and ever'" (Hebrews 1:8)

- The Holy Spirit is God: "Then Peter said, 'Ananias, how is it that Satan has so filled your heart that you have lied to the Holy Spirit ... You have not lied just to men but to God" (Acts 5:3–4)

- There is only one God: "Hear, O Israel: The Lord our God, the Lord is one" (Deuteronomy 6:4)

I must admit, I never thought the Trinity had much personal application. The Trinity seemed like a nice theological concept, nothing more. I studied it in college, mentioned the Trinity in sermons, and of course, believed it. But a concept that might transform me? No way.

My views have changed. Lately, I've found myself meditating in wonder and complete amazement. Here are some of my thoughts:

- I love and serve a God who exists in perfect relationship.
- God is not a lone ranger. He exists in community.
- His communion with the other members of the Godhead is my model to follow.

The Father, Son, and Holy Spirit reside in every believer. God's very nature, therefore, is to guide his children to form relationships with others. God says in Genesis 1:26, "Let us make mankind in our image, in our likeness . . ." Notice, the plurality of "let us" and "our image." God is transforming us into his own relational image. Larry Crabb writes,

> We were designed by our Trinitarian God (who is Himself a group of three persons in profound relationship with each other) to live in relationship. Without it, we die. It's that simple. Without a community where we know, explore, discover, and touch one another, we experience isolation and despair that drive us in wrong directions that corrupt our efforts to live meaningfully and to love well.[40]

Christ's goal while on earth was to mold and shape his disciples to be like the Trinity. He journeyed with them for three years to demonstrate and teach them about love and community. Molding and shaping them as a community was the key component of their training. Jesus had a huge challenge to unite such a diverse group. He brought together disciples who were temperamental and easily offended. They often saw each other as competitors, and it was not easy for them to wash each other's feet (John 13:14).

Jesus often pointed to the unity within the Trinity as a model for his disciples to follow. Notice how Jesus describes his relationship to the Father:

. . . that all of them may be one, Father, just as you are in me and I am in you. May they also be in us so that the world may believe that you have sent me. I have given them the glory that you gave me, that they may be one as we are one (John 17:21–22).

And Jesus succeeded as he patiently helped them to understand the importance of unity and love for one another.

Granted, the disciples were with Jesus in the flesh. We are not. But God has promised his Holy Spirit to help us become like the Trinity and then in turn to prioritize our own intimate relationships. The bottom line is that we need the Trinity working through us to succeed with those closest to us.

God helps us see his presence in others and to love them like He does. He transforms us to act like him. Acting independently goes against his character. Community, in fact, is the very nature of God. He will stir us to love one another, serve one another, wait on one another, and walk in humility with one another. Jesus wants us to have success with those closest to us. It starts with those who we know best and then extends to those who don't know us as well.

Spouse

The first link in my inner circle is my relationship with Celyce, whom I married on February 13, 1988. She knows how I react to life's circumstances. She knows the *why* behind my life and ministry, and her counsel to me is based on patterns and experiences that only she knows. God uses her to sharpen me, and I do the same with her. We are still constantly fine-tuning each other. We overcome conflict, relax, envision, make decisions, and care for each other.

My Christian character is first tested in my relationship with her and only later with others. I need to succeed in this relationship to truly live in victory in the Christian life. Why? Because she knows me intimately. She knows whether I'm obeying God's Word, walking in love, and becoming like Jesus. And the good news is that I've seen a lot of progress. I've had to confess a lot of sin, but Jesus is making me more like him.

My desire is to be the best husband possible and to develop the deepest, most intimate relationship with Celyce. She is my ministry. She's not a part of my ministry.

I'm saddened to think that during certain periods in our marriage, I acted as if the main goal in my life was personal success and that marriage was for support of my own good. I expected her to "fall in line" and help me in my ministry. God has slowly, graciously shown me that Celyce is my number one ministry. Therefore, the chief questions I need to ask are:

- Does she believe we're improving in our marriage?
- Are we having fun together?
- Am I spending quality time with her?
- Are we growing in our friendship?
- Am I sensitive to seeing things through her eyes?

We must diligently work on our relationship. Conflict can spring up anytime. In fact, conflict is a key part of the maturing package—learning to be like Jesus. The intensity of marriage brings those conflicts to a new level. While we have each other, we need to be constantly growing in our relationship with each other.

In marriage, we're both learning to ask God to give us the grace to apologize, forgive, confess our own sin, and then move on. We rejoice that our love and relationship is growing deeper all the time. I've had to confess and deal with the bondage of anger. I've had to come to the point to admit that anger is always a sin—at least in my relationship with Celyce.

God might be using your spouse to drive you to your knees. You might have to ask God for grace and forgiveness. Believe that God is molding and shaping you. This is part of the growth package—the way that God is making you more like him.

Some have experienced a broken inner circle through divorce, betrayal, death, or some other tragedy. If this has been your experience, God is able to start the process over and give you a new inner circle. You might have failed in your relationship with your children, behaved badly toward your parents, or disassociated with close friends for whatever reason. No matter what the situation, God's grace makes us complete. And he delights in reshaping our lives.

God's grace takes us where we are and moves us forward. C. S. Lewis once said that God will reward us according to the progress we've made from where we started. Billy Graham started farther ahead than most people, having been raised in a godly Christian family. Others have started from a broken home but have made huge strides forward.

Mario, a friend of mine, was a successful pastor in Long Island, New York. His church grew quite large. Then his inner circle began to unravel. His wife, diagnosed with bipolar disease, began having an intimate relationship with another woman.

Mario tried everything to save his marriage, including months of counseling under the watchful eye of his Baptist superintendent. His wife continued to pursue her lesbian relationship and eventually divorced Mario. His church asked him to leave. You can imagine the depths of darkness Mario faced at that time. Thankfully, his children, seeing their dad's godly responses throughout the crisis, remained faithful to Jesus.

Eventually, Mario remarried a godly woman who had experienced similar marriage upheaval. He began working in the secular world, but the call to ministry tugged at his heart, and years later, he answered God's call to return to the pastorate when an evangelical church in Texas hired Mario after examining his rebuilt inner world. The church saw how God had used Mario's tragedy to make him stronger.

I'm in contact now with Mario on a regular basis. He has a deeper compassion for people. He's walked with God through the valley and has come out stronger and wiser. He's able to help others through their difficult times because God has helped him.

Tragedies strike families and marriages all the time. The good news is that God rebuilds inner circles, like he did with Mario. Christ can completely turn a dark situation into a shining example.

God is the God of hope. He loves to display his strength in weaknesses and failures. He wants to make you a relational disciple who will have an impact on the lives of many. But you must start from a secure foundation. God is the one who takes us and compels us forward. He leads us into the future.

Family

I shared a meal with a missionary who told me his dad, an international minister, stopped his ministry for one year to spend time with him during his troubled years. I admire this father's commitment to place the well-being of his child above his own ministerial success. Sadly, many have not. They've placed their own success over relationship with their children.

I believe the highest goal for our children is that they would love the Lord God with all their heart, soul, mind, and strength (Luke 10:27). This should be the greatest desire of parents for their children—to accurately pass the baton of the Christian faith to them, and that they would remain committed disciples of Christ. Granted, this is our goal but it's often messy and children don't always behave as we want. The good news is that when we train our children in the way they should go, even if they go astray, we can trust that they will come back.

I'm convinced that the family devotional time is the best time for parents to nurture children in the ways of God and really prepare them for life with Christ. Having a quiet time with the kids doesn't ensure that they will follow Jesus later. It only reflects the priorities of the parents to prioritize godliness. Parents have a golden opportunity to train children in the ways of Jesus when they are young.

Growing healthy kids isn't only about shared devotional time. It's also about friendship, fun, and spontaneous activity. Plato once wrote, "You can learn more about a man in an hour of play than in a year of conversation."[41] Taking a full day off is essential—both for parents and family members. It gives the family a chance to have fun, gather strength, and face the week with new vigor. And it helps the family build and maintain strong relationships.

Children feel cared for and loved when their father and mother live in harmony. We know from experience that when we, as husband and wife, are doing well, our children feel secure. When I make my wife feel special, my kids honor me in a special way. I believe a successful relationship between husband and wife is half the battle when it comes to proper child-rearing. The husband and wife relationship is the glue that makes other relationships work. The greatest thing a father can do for his children is to love his wife.

One Christian friend who suffered a divorce recently recalled his son asking during the divorce proceedings, "Where is God in all this, Dad?" His son still hasn't recovered. The glue of marriage, which was supposed to help this boy grow in his relationship with God, lost its grip.

God is looking for godly offspring as parents prioritize each other and their children (Malachi 2:13–16). God desires for kids to see community lived out between father and mother. When this is not the case, children develop insecurity. Often children of divorced parents experience bitterness because of the vague hopelessness they feel about their own prospects of developing close relationships with a future spouse.

I'm constantly reminded that my kids are God's instruments to make me more like Jesus. Michael Farris, an educator and author who successfully raised three daughters, wrote a book called *What a Daughter Needs from Her Dad*. He says:

> From a very early age your daughter will know when you have
> made the wrong decision, snapped to an inappropriate judgment
> . . . A father who refuses to admit a mistake or to work at changing
> poor, immature behavior reaps a daughter who refuses to trust him
> . . . Your reliability is actually enhanced when you are willing to admit
> to the evident fact that you have made a mistake.[42]

My constant prayer is that I would admit my mistakes when
my children point them out. Acknowledgment and confession are
far better choices than justification and rejection. They also build
healthy respect. I've acted so immaturely at times, bursting out in
anger, behaving impatiently, and not being sensitive. I've found
it far better to humble myself, apologize, listen to my kids, and
then ask God to work deeply within me. God wants to mold me
through these situations. Kids see what's truly happening in the
heart of parents. Children are like mirrors that point out weaknesses, joys, and victories.

We live in victory as we allow the Holy Spirit to mold and shape
us through those who are closest to us. Yes, these relationships
challenge us the most, but they also help us develop Christian character and to become more like Jesus.

Friends

Jesus made friendships a top priority. He enjoyed going to the
home of Mary, Martha, and Lazarus. This was probably a place
where Jesus could relax and feel like a normal human. Christ's disciples were also his friends. In fact, he told his disciples that he
considered them friends, as opposed to servants (John 15:15).

Friendship was also important to the apostle Paul. Notice what
he says in 2 Corinthians 2:12–13: "Now when I went to Troas to
preach the gospel of Christ and found that the Lord had opened
a door for me, I still had no peace of mind, because I did not find
my brother Titus there. So I said good-bye to them and went on to

Macedonia." Although preaching the gospel was Paul's priority, he also understood the need for friendship.

We all need a close friend—someone with whom we can share intimate details of our lives. The authors Will Miller and Glenn Sparks of *Refrigerator Rights* believe that too many people look to their spouses to fulfill all their emotional needs, putting a tremendous strain on the marriage. Spouses need additional friendships outside of the marriage. Granted, close friends are hard to find and harder to keep. One of my closest friends died of a brain tumor. We had cultivated a close friendship for almost thirty-plus years before he died. That type of friendship is hard to recreate.

A few years ago, I ministered in Hong Kong and afterward, toured the city with a group from Japan. Doug, a career missionary to Japan, and I talked about his unique training ministry around the world.

"As I speak to leaders within Japan and in other countries, the one common denominator is the lack of friendship," he said. "Busy leaders are often very lonely. They have few people to turn to in times of need."

We both acknowledged that it's not just a leadership problem. It's a problem we all face, especially in Western culture. We consume our extra time with work and don't take time to establish deep friendships.

Friendship is not a one-way street. People who only want to talk without also listening, don't make good friends. Kevin Strong, the one who died of cancer, was one of my best friends. Kevin always did two things well. First, he shared what was happening in his life. Second, he asked great questions. He practiced active listening (e.g., "so I hear you saying") and then asked additional questions to draw out meaning.

My advice is to find one or two solid friends of the same gender. Open your heart and schedule to those people—both fun and spontaneous time, as well as serious sharing time. Establish regular contact with them. Practice self-disclosure, knowing that one of the key ingredients of a true friend is transparency. And don't forget to pray for one another. Be transparent. Share what's really on your heart. Go deep.

My wife, Celyce, and I have some very close friends with whom we meet each year for about five days. When we are together, we laugh, confess, and hold each other accountable. They also know us intimately, having been our closest friends for about thirty-six years.

Living in victory with our friends is essential because they know us over time. They are committed to us over the long haul and speak the truth in love. Proverbs 18:24 says, "One who has unreliable friends soon comes to ruin, but there is a friend who sticks closer than a brother." Those are the type of friends we need.

The Journey

If you don't have an inner circle, ask Jesus to help you form one. He will direct you to one or more people with whom you can have a close friendship and accountability relationship. The key is to find people who know you well enough to hold you accountable. You will grow in relationship with these people, and you'll reflect Jesus Christ more fully as you fine-tune each other.

The Trinity created humans to live in relationship, just like he dwells in perpetual community with the other members of the Godhead. In the beginning, God understood that it was not good for his human creation to be alone. He created a spouse, family, and friends for us to have people with whom we can share our life's journey.

We all face emotional, spiritual, and physical struggles. But along the way, we look to those who are closest to us to provide counsel, encouragement, and assistance in our spiritual growth. They are the ones with whom we can rejoice, weep, and share transparently. In other words, they are the ones who matter most.

They also know whether we are growing in the Christian faith—or going backward. We can appear to be doing great before the crowd, or even with those at work, but we will not mislead those closest to us. They know us intimately and will mold us and shape us while we do the same for them.

As we journey with those closest to us and allow them to mold and shape us, we'll become more like the Trinity. And that's the goal of the Christian life—to be like the God who made us and called us to glorify his name.

Points to Consider

- What is the main principle you've learned from this chapter? How will you apply it?
- How would you describe your relationships in your inner circle?
- What can you do to improve your relationship with those closest to you?
- How does your relationship with the Trinity help you to prioritize those closest to you?

Get Connected with God's Family

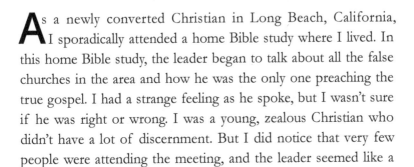

As a newly converted Christian in Long Beach, California, I sporadically attended a home Bible study where I lived. In this home Bible study, the leader began to talk about all the false churches in the area and how he was the only one preaching the true gospel. I had a strange feeling as he spoke, but I wasn't sure if he was right or wrong. I was a young, zealous Christian who didn't have a lot of discernment. But I did notice that very few people were attending the meeting, and the leader seemed like a lone ranger.

The next Sunday, I attended the local Foursquare Church in downtown Long Beach. Pastor Billy Adams, an established and respected pastor for many, many years, preached consistently from the Bible. Pastor Billy was preaching that Sunday in 2 Peter about the dangers of false prophets. The Spirit of God spoke to me that the home Bible study teacher was one of those false prophets and that I needed to stay close to Pastor Billy's teaching and this local Foursquare church. I never went back to that home Bible study.

Years later, while still living in Long Beach, California, I was part of a ministry that spun out of control due to the ungodly lifestyle of the founding pastor. Many left the ministry and their faith in Christ. Once again, I needed the local church. Chuck Smith, pastor of nearby Calvary Chapel, came to my rescue. I began attending Calvary Chapel as well as listening to Chuck Smith's teaching tapes. The preaching of God's Word guided my path and helped me to avoid error and false doctrine. I also found fellowship at Calvary Chapel and eventually started my own home group, which was related to Calvary Chapel. Once again, God used the local church to guide my paths.

Me and God Christianity

Many people believe they don't need the local church. They are like my friend, Jim, who prayed the "sinner's prayer." I had been witnessing to Jim for a long time, and he now was a Christian—or so I thought. Over the months, I noticed that Jim did not like to attend church, telling me that he was a very private person and didn't like to share his life with other people.

After many months, I felt the need to challenge his individualistic thinking. I said to him, "Those who know Jesus are willing to have others hold them accountable. They don't hold on to a privatized religion and their own personal faith." My words hit a wall. Jim didn't mind hearing about Jesus and was willing to even "accept Christ." But to become a responsible member of the body of Christ was far, far from his mind.

Jim, like so many others, had bought into a privatized view of Christianity—me and God. Author and pastor, Tod Bolsinger, heard this individualistic message while growing up. He writes,

> What most of us heard in those kinds of messages is that we can have a personal and private relationship with Christ. I remember the youth leader giving an invitation and saying, "There is nothing to join, you don't have to be a church member. It's just about having a relationship with Jesus." And I wanted that. Not church, but Jesus. Shortly after I committed my life to following Christ, I bought a T-shirt that said "JC and me." It was a not-so-subtle way of sharing my faith, and it described my new-found belief perfectly. This wasn't my parents' religion, this wasn't about tradition or ritual, it was about "JC and me"—a sentiment that always sounds good until you start reading the Bible.[43]

Notice the last part of Bolsinger's words, "a sentiment that always sounds good until you start reading the Bible." What might sound cool in an individualistic culture is very foreign to a biblical view of community. Too often, we've acted like we don't need to congregate with other believers.

The resistance to faithfully meet with other believers on a regular basis is not a new problem. The same tendency was happening back in the New Testament church as well. To confront this dilemma, the writer of Hebrews said, "And let us consider how we may spur one another on toward love and good deeds, not giving up meeting together, as some are in the habit of doing, but encouraging one another—and all the more as you see the Day approaching" (Hebrews 10:25). The human propensity is to resist accountability and to only answer to ourselves. But the New Testament tells us often that we need each other (you'll find more than fifty "one-another" references).

We need to be involved in the local church to live in true victory.

What Is the Church?

One denomination required a church to have a building before calling it a church. A church planter within this denomination wrote an entire Ph.D. dissertation to show that the church of Jesus Christ didn't need a building to be called an official church. This church planter's plan was to start a small group, multiply the group, and eventually meet in a larger facility. He wanted his denomination to recognize that the initial small group was a biblically functioning church.

So what is a true church? Is it necessary for a church to have:

- A building?
- A pulpit?
- A certain number of people?
- Land?

These things might be included in a church, but they are not the church. The Bible uses the term *ecclesia,* gathering of believers, to describe the church. This word refers to those who are *called out* by God. Paul uses *ecclesia* to describe the house church as well as the larger gathering. For example, in 1 Corinthians 1:2, Paul addresses the entire church of Corinth (*ecclesia*), but then in 1 Corinthians 16:19, he writes to the church in the house of Aquila and Priscilla (*ecclesia*). The same word is used for both the larger gathering and smaller one.

The church is a group of believers gathered under the lordship of Jesus and God-appointed leaders to grow in Christ's likeness, hear and obey God's Word, and participate in the sacraments (baptism—Matthew 28:19 and the Lord's Supper—Matthew 26:26–28).[44]

The local church meets regularly in time and space. I have problems with those who water down the definition of a church by saying that attending an occasional Christian concert or turning on the TV to listen to a preacher is the same as involvement in a local church. The local church, rather, is a physical gathering of believers at a city level or a house church level (Acts 12:12; Romans 16:3–5; 1 Corinthians 16:19; Colossians 4:15; Philemon 2).

Christ's church is not complicated. He created it to be nimble and reproducible in every nation on the earth—not just those with enough money to acquire parking lots and build sanctuaries. God calls believers to be part of a local church to help them grow in their faith and become more like Jesus.

More Than a Human Institution

Many people look at the local church as optional. If they have time, they will participate in a local church. If not, they won't.

Scripture tells us a different story. Jesus is the head of the church (Ephesians 1:22), and Paul even calls it Christ's body (1 Corinthians 12:12–26). One phrase used to describe the local church is the *bride of Christ* (Revelation 19:7) which highlights just how special the church is to Jesus. God has ordained the local church as the place where we grow to become more like Jesus in the presence of and fellowship with others. God has also raised up divinely appointed leaders in the local church to watch over us, guide us, and to know us personally.

If we're going to live in victory, we need to stay connected to the local church. Here are a few reasons:

- The local church helps us to stay on the right path. If we are hearing God's Word preached on a regular basis, we are far more likely to follow the narrow path the Bible lays out. Satan is always trying to thwart believers from God's ways (1 Peter 5:8–9).

- The local church helps us build like-minded relationships. Not all friendships are good ones. Relationships built in a biblically based local church encourage us to live for God. Being involved in a local church is a key place to develop the intimate relationships I talked about in the previous chapter.

- Pastoral care. God calls pastors and church leaders to care for believers in good times and bad (e.g., sickness, marriage, and so forth).

- Discipleship happens in the context of the local church.

After Christ's resurrection, the word *disciple* was replaced by words such as *believer, saint, Christian, brother* or *sister* in Christ. Why? Because after Pentecost, God established the church, the gathering of believers, to be the main place where discipleship occurred. Rather than becoming disciples through the effort of one person, the early Christians were molded and shaped by the Spirit of God, working through Christ's church.

The early church followed Christ's pattern and changed the world house by house. Those house churches celebrated together in a local gathering (Acts 5:42; 20:20). Michael Wilkens says,

> Discipling today is always undertaken as an outgrowth of the life of the church, whereas prior to Pentecost it occurred with Jesus personally. . . We may go so far as to say that in many ways, discipleship is the overall goal of the church, including evangelism, nurturing, fellowship, leadership, worship, etc.[45]

God chose the church to make disciples—both today and in New Testament times. He has ordained the local church to renew our vision and get us ready for the second coming of Jesus Christ. Ricky Jones, church planter in Oklahoma, says,

> I want you to understand that being a part of the universal church without submitting to a local church is not possible, biblical, or healthy.
>
> First, it's simply not possible. To imply you can be part of the greater community without first being part of the smaller is not logical. You cannot be part of Rotary International without also being part of a local chapter. You cannot be part of the universal human family without first being part of a small immediate family.
>
> Second, it's not biblical. Every letter in the New Testament assumes Christians are members of local churches. The letters themselves are addressed to local churches. They teach us how to get along with other members, how to encourage the weak within the church, how to conduct ourselves at church, and what to do with unrepentant sinners in the church. They command us to submit to our elders, and encourage us to go to our elders to pray. All these things are impossible if you aren't a member of a local church. (See 1 and 2 Corinthians, James, Ephesians, 1 and 2 Timothy, and 1 Peter for references.)[46]

A dynamic local church should include the opportunity to be known in a smaller group as well as to gather in a larger group for worship. When Jesus left earth, he told his followers to make disciples of all nations (Matthew 28:18–20). Those first disciples met in homes and gathered in larger groups whenever possible (Acts 2:42–46).

Be Known in a Small Group

Billy Graham once said, "If you find a perfect church don't join it: You'd spoil it."[47] The perfect church doesn't exist. That's because the perfect person doesn't exist, and churches are made up of imperfect people. Yet, God has chosen to work through imperfect people. Our closest friends overlook our imperfections. This holds true for families and churches. You'll need to learn to look past personalities who rub you wrong and people you disagree with. God will mold and shape you in the process.

Some people jump from church to church before they get to know anyone intimately. They avoid smaller churches where the members know each other in favor of larger churches where they can avoid relationships—slipping in and out before they get to know people intimately. Avoid this. Get to know others and let them get to know you.

Unlike the way we view church today, the New Testament passages were primarily written to house churches where believers met to participate in the Lord's Supper, minister through the gifts of the Spirit, reflect on Scripture, and build each other up.

The best place, in fact, to experience church is in a small group of three to fifteen people. After all, the New Testament movement was a house to house movement (Acts 2:42–46; 5:42; 20:20).

Jesus chose a small group of twelve to disciple his own followers. He knew that the small group was the best way to interact and practice learning and transparency. True Christian fellowship is never secretive. Rather, it's honest, open, and free from lies and obscurity. The apostle John, writing to a house church says, ". . . if we walk in the light, as he is in the light, we have *fellowship* with one another, and the blood of Jesus, his Son, purifies us from all sin" (1 John 1:7). In the early house church meetings, each person was encouraged to share freely, as James says, "Therefore confess your sins to each other and pray for each other so that you may be healed" (James 5:16).

The early house churches multiplied throughout the Roman Empire, practicing both evangelism and open hospitality. New people joined their fellowship because of its open family atmosphere, and the house churches grew and multiplied. As Jesus transformed people, they behaved differently, and friends and neighbors were drawn to this new transformed community. Their changed lifestyles spilled over into the community around them, and at the same time, their intimate fellowship increased. People could see the changes up close as community life was lived out in the open. The home groups were both relationally based but also very effective in outreach. When God is at work, both of these things happen.

Jesus cultivates a deep love in our lives for one another as well as for those who still need him. I might not get along with everyone in the small group, but this is an opportunity to trust in God for supernatural love. In such circumstances, I need to say, "Lord, give me strength to love that person. Help me to overlook the aspect of his or her personality that grates on me."

Celyce and I have actively been involved in small groups for many years, and we still are. We both realize that we need the intimate accountability of others, a place to share what's happening in our own lives, and the prayers of God's people. God also wants to use us to speak into the lives of others. We are convinced that small group involvement is a non-negotiable aspect of the Christian life.

The Larger Gathering

Both the larger gathering and the small group gathering are very important. Paul preached publicly and from house to house (Acts

20:20). In the book of Acts, believers often met in the large group and the small one (Acts 2:42–46). In fact, small groups function best when they are connected to a larger gathering with specific overseers.

We read in Acts 2:42 that the earliest believers in Jerusalem devoted themselves to the "apostles' teaching." Effective churches have regular celebration services in which all the small groups come together to hear specific teaching from the Bible. In the celebration, those who are called to preach and teach God's Word may do so. Many don't understand the awesome responsibility placed on pastors. Scripture in Ephesians 4:11–13, implies that:

> It is Christ himself who gave the apostles, the prophets, the evangelists, the pastors and teachers, to equip his people for works of service, so that the body of Christ may be built up until we all reach unity in the faith and in the knowledge of the Son of God and become mature, attaining to the whole measure of the fullness of Christ.

God has placed ministers in his body to help believers grow so that they might be involved in the church's ministry. Part of this fine-tuning is to help believers stay on God's path and not stray into enemy territory. Pastors and teachers are supernaturally gifted to teach and apply God's Word to help believers grow in their faith. They help believers walk in victory by pointing out God's scriptural plan for their lives. They guide God's people through the straight and narrow path (Acts 20:28). They help believers to walk in victory by teaching and reminding them of God's wonderful promises (Acts 20:32).

The larger gathering is also a time for leaders to cast vision and direction with everyone present. Under Christ's authority, the church moves together to reach a needy world and to make disciples of all people (Matthew 28:18–20). Jesus doesn't have a plan B, although many have tried to justify a way to avoid church. Avoiding God's plan for the local church is a recipe for disaster and defeat.

Victory, on the other hand, comes when believers move together in both small and large groups through the local church.

The Spiritual Family

For many people from non-Christian homes and families, the church will become even closer than their own families. The love of Jesus working through brothers and sisters produces a love that can only be found within Christ's church. The work of Christ through a community of believers helps us renew our vision, keeps us on the right path, and sharpens our spiritual walk. We can also share our burdens and receive help along the way (Galatians 6:1–2).

The Bible is full of references about God being our Father, other Christians our brothers and sisters, and the church being God's family. I believe, in fact, that the clearest and most prominent image of the church is God's family. [48] Joseph Hellerman writes in his book *When the Church Was a Family,*

> In the New Testament era a person was not saved for the sole purpose of enjoying a personal relationship with God. Indeed, the phrase "personal relationship with God" is found nowhere in the Bible. According to the New Testament, a person is saved to community. Salvation included membership in God's group. We are saved "into one body," . . . when we get a new Father we also get a new set of brothers and sisters. In Scripture salvation is a community-creating event. [49]

While we need to teach that each person receives Christ's salvation individually, we must not promote salvation apart from Christian growth. And this takes place in the family of God, Christ's church.

My own home church is Nuevo Amanecer (New Beginning) in Los Angeles, California. Many come from different countries in Latin America. They've left their home cultures and families behind to live in the U.S. Many of them view the church as their new family. They eagerly open their homes for small group meetings and participate in the larger gatherings. Food is always a delight as they experience the family of God together.

For many people, however, any reference to the church as a family is seen as negative. The high rate of divorce, the proliferation of abuse within family systems, and the absenteeism that defines much modern-day parenting sets a stage for many in our churches to resist any kind of familial experience. They do not want to repeat an experience of abandonment, misunderstanding, and pain from their past.

I believe the best remedy to help new believers and new members experience the church as a family is to get them connected to a small group as soon as possible.

Church as a family also means we welcome those who are lonely and isolated and do not have a family. The new family that Jesus came to establish was not based on blood relationships, but on a new spiritual reality. Jesus welcomed all people to join that new family. We must do the same. One of the main reasons the early church grew so rapidly was because it welcomed newcomers into the extended family, and then continued the process of multiplication to make sure there was room for everyone in God's family. House church extension was the natural step to reach more people for Jesus.

We must encourage church members to reach out to people who desperately need community and a place to belong. This can be done through special outreach events in both the small group as well as the larger church gathering.

Leaders must model what they are asking others to do by participating in small groups and relational evangelism. One practical way to do this is to ask key leaders to model family life, either by leading a small group or participating in one. This will strengthen the family emphasis when the church sees the leaders practicing what they're preaching.

If you're not involved in a local church, ask God to show you the right one for you. If you're in one, ask God to help make you a servant to others. Living in victory involves being accountable to others under God-ordained leadership through the local church.

Points to Consider

- What is the main principle you've learned from this chapter? How will you apply it?

- What is your current level of involvement in a local church?

- How has Jesus used the local church in your own life? The life of your family?

- What can you do to prioritize your local church?

Spiritual Truth #6

Make Time for Rest

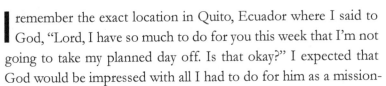

I remember the exact location in Quito, Ecuador where I said to God, "Lord, I have so much to do for you this week that I'm not going to take my planned day off. Is that okay?" I expected that God would be impressed with all I had to do for him as a missionary and that he'd give me a green light to avoid taking my day off. Rather, I sensed a gentle, loving admonition:

"Joel, I'm more concerned about you and your rest, rather than all you can do for me."

That day, God was inviting me to the discipline of rest. God was asking me to spend time with him, to renew my mind and body, and come away from the daily grind in order to love him and seek his face.

And something very interesting happened as a result of that experience. I began to realize that as I faithfully took a day off, I would get more and better work done for the rest of the week. After my day off, I felt rested and renewed to face the challenges with far more vigor and effectiveness. When I tried to fill seven days with work, I slugged through those days on very low energy and accomplished little. Far from being a hindrance, I discovered that taking a day off helped me to live victoriously each day of the week.

Resistance to Rest

Over the years, I've noticed a resistance to taking a day off. The response goes like this, "Oh, a day off? Certainly not. I'm too busy doing God's work. Vacations? No way, I have so much to do for the Lord." When people say things like this, they assume that others will be impressed by their hard work and pat them on their back for not being lazy or slothful. And certainly, people who say such things don't fall into the lazy category.

Others don't take a day off because they want to make more money. And yes, we have to pay the bills, rent, and provide for our families. But most do not stop when those needs are met. In her classic text, *The Overworked American*, Juliet Schor examines why, with increased productivity, people are working more and more. The answer? They must pay for their equally increased consumerism, which has led to fewer and fewer hours devoted to play and leisure.[50] They work beyond the expected norm because they want more.

Still others don't take a day off because they believe they are indispensable. I was in a church where the pastor's wife boasted that she never took a day off because so many things had to get done. She was the mover and shaker in the church, and I noticed a spirit of striving that primarily exuded from her actions. She was very articulate but also very demanding and even harsh.

She manifested an unhealthiness in her life and actions that negatively affected the entire church. Others felt they were never doing enough and had to be busy to be accepted. I felt a performance pressure in that church and realized that her pressure was making the church emotionally unhealthy. She embraced the notion that unless she worked unceasingly, the church would not succeed.

In contrast, the God who made us asks us to rest. Victory in the Christian life flows from a rested mind, soul, and body.

The God of Rest

God loves rest and delights when his creation follows his eternal principles. Throughout the Old and New Testaments, we discover a God who wanted and even commanded his people to rest. He said to his people,

> "Remember the Sabbath day, to keep it holy. Six days you shall labor, and do all your work, but the seventh day is a Sabbath to the Lord your God. On it you shall not do any work, you, or your son, or your daughter, your male servant, or your female servant, or your livestock, or the sojourner who is within your gates. For in six days the Lord made heaven and earth, the sea, and all that is in them, and rested on the seventh day. Therefore the Lord blessed the Sabbath day and made it holy" (Exodus 20:8–11 ESV).

God wired his creation to only effectively work and produce six days a week (Genesis 2:2). He repeatedly tells his people to rest for their own good. Rather than restricting them, he knows they can't live in victory when they're tired and sluggish. Rest gives new strength.

Rest is a principle, rather than a particular day. Some groups today highlight one specific day and become dogmatic about it. They criticize anyone else who doesn't rest on that one day. I've seen signs along the road that proclaim, "Obey God by keeping the Sabbath Day." To these people, Saturday is holy and those who don't practice the Saturday observance are living in disobedience.

The actual Sabbath, however, was given as a sign between Israel and Jehovah (Ezekiel 20:12). Since Christ's death and resurrection, we are now in a new era of grace in which God has a relationship with all who call on his name. Israel will always be special before God, and he has a special calling for them. But Christ's church extends beyond one nation or people. All who call on Jesus as Lord and Savior form part of Christ's church.

The early church saw themselves as the new people of God. They chose Sunday to worship in memory of Jesus Christ who rose again on the first day of the week (1 Corinthians 16:2). The concept of the "Lord's Day" (Revelation 1:10) appears throughout the New Testament, and it refers to Sunday. The early believers celebrated their new status, as opposed to the Jewish observance of Saturday, by worshipping on Sunday. For example, in Acts 20:7, we read, "On the first day of the week we came together to break bread."

And even though the early church celebrated on Sunday, their practice was not supposed to usher in a new set of rules. Rather, it was the day to focus on the Lord—to love and adore the risen one and enter his presence. Jesus himself said that the day of rest (Sabbath) was created for the benefit of God's people and not the other way around (Mark 2:27).

Jesus would often call people to the principle rather than the structure. He did work on the Sabbath and the religious leaders judged him, but he reminded them that the Sabbath was made for man, not man for the Sabbath. In other words, Sabbath rest is the point, not the actual day (Matthew 12:3–8). God created the rest day to bless people, not to place a set of legalistic rules on them.

The movie *Chariots of Fire* tells the story of Eric Liddell and the Olympic games. Liddell refused to run on Sunday because he felt he would be violating the principle of the Sabbath. Little believed that Sunday was God's specific day of rest. He believed that running on that day would have violated God's law.

I honor Liddell for his convictions. He couldn't run on Sunday in good conscience. But I don't agree. The principle of rest supersedes the exact day. Sunday is not a sign between God and the church in the same way the Sabbath was between Jehovah and the nation of Israel. The principle of resting one day, however, is firmly embedded throughout Scripture.

The day is not critical. In fact, many people must work on Sunday. And what about pastors? Sunday is their busiest day. I really doubt that a pastor can truly rest on Sunday. When we grasp that rest is the critical factor, not the day, we can then understand the reasons behind taking a day off:

- to worship and obey God

- to receive the needed healing in body and soul
- to change our pace to get a better perspective on life
- to spend time with family

Understanding the *why* will motivate us to take a day off. Everyone could believe that they do not have enough time to take a day off. We're all extremely busy. To move from theory and idealism to practice involves saying, "God, you have placed the rest principle in Scripture, and I'm simply going to obey you and take a day off."

The principle is that God knows what we need, and he invites us to come away one day per week for rest and renewal. It's for our own good. When fully rested, we'll be more tranquil, directed, and productive. We will live in victory.

Just Stop

Nike is famous for the slogan *Just Do it.* For some people, the slogan *Just Stop* is desperately needed. *Just stop.* Cease from work. It might be hard but when it happens, healing and then victory happens. Many people can't stop working. They want to just do a little more. But God says "stop." If you know what's good for you, "stop." Rest. Come away from work.

In the long run, those who rest well will get a lot more done, and the quality of that work will be far better. When a person is running on empty, he or she can accomplish very little. Resting one day per week energizes believers spiritually, emotionally, and physically. Marva J. Dawn, author of *Keeping the Sabbath Wholly*, writes,

> To cease working on the Sabbath means to quit laboring at anything that is work. Activity that is enjoyable and freeing and not undertaken for the purpose of accomplishment qualifies as acceptable for Sabbath time.[51]

We live in a 24/7 world where people work constantly, have continuous stimulation, and never-ending social interaction. At one time, many countries and cultures promoted one day of rest.

Now Saturday and Sunday are anything but quiet. Sports, shopping, and even business activity flourishes on the weekend. Pastor A. J. Swoboda, writes in *Subversive Sabbath,*

> America was once a nation built on Sabbath. Tilden Edwards recalls walking around New York City as a child on a Sabbath day, finding it completely quiet—everyone was worshiping together at church. Until fairly recently, people did not need to be as intentional about rest as we do now. Sabbath, in large part, was legislated in the United States.[52]

Because the culture no longer encourages rest, people must have the inner conviction that taking a day off is valuable and essential.

Rest helps us humble ourselves and to remember that life is more than work. It's saying, "God, I trust in you despite what I think needs to be done. I lay down what I think I must do and trust in you for what you know I need to do." Resting one day is seeing beyond hard work and developing a relationship with God. One key aspect of rest is the renewal and strength that leads to greater productivity and fruit.

I overworked one spring to the point of exhaustion. I didn't faithfully keep my day off, didn't take care of my body, and eventually caught bronchitis. I had a teaching commitment at the time that I couldn't cancel.

I'll never forget those sleepless nights wheezing and coughing, knowing that I had to teach the next day. As I look back at those exhausting days, I now realize I tried to cram way too much work into a limited time period and ended up imbalanced. In my desire to fulfill certain goals, I didn't keep my regular day off, so my family time suffered, and I didn't spend quality time with the Lord.

The "school of hard knocks," a lot of challenging input from friends, and time in the Scriptures has changed me. There is a reason, after all, that the principle of setting aside one day to rest permeates Scripture. I learned that I must maintain certain priorities in my life if I wanted to have victory over the long haul. And one of those principles was taking a full day of rest. I needed to simply stop and prioritize time with my Creator.

A pastoral team once came over to my house for ministry consulting. We spent the day talking about their church and the next steps they needed to take for vitality in their church and small groups. Near the end of our time together, the pastor started telling me about his counseling ministry and how people needed him 24/7 for counseling. He had to be available all the time, day and night. And, often, this was above and beyond his ministry in the church because many of these people were outside his own church community.

I asked him whether he was getting a day off to come away and rest. I expected him to say yes, but rather, he came back and said, "No, I cannot. These people need me all the time. I have to be available all the time."

I pushed back but realized the discussion was becoming heated in his insistence that he needed to always be available to these people. I changed the subject, knowing he had strong convictions.

The Pastoral staff left that meeting and I didn't hear from them for several years. Then the associate who had accompanied the pastor that day told me that the pastor had died a couple of years after that meeting. Was he exhausted? I'm not sure. I just know that this young pastor (maybe forty-five at the time) had died within two years of my conversation with him concerning resting.

I often hear, "Joel, I like what you're saying, but you don't know my schedule. I just can't do what you're asking." I do realize that each situation is different. But is it necessary to work seven days per week? Ask God to give you wisdom on how to separate one day to rest. I believe he will. Be creative. He'll show you how to arrange for a day of rest.

Better Results

Peter Scazzero admits in his book, *The Emotionally Healthy Church,* that his own church had become toxic in its quest for growth and success. He realized that the church was prioritizing production over rest and numbers over discipleship. Yes, they did produce numerical growth, but sin and strife accompanied those numbers and the church suffered as a result.

Thankfully, Scazzero turned the church in a new direction and began to prioritize healthy living among the members. Among other spiritual principles, Scazzero required that the church leadership take a day of rest. They modeled the priority of rest to the remainder of the church, and the church became far healthier and more productive as a result.

People need to realize that they will have far better health and victory if they will simply dedicate one day per week to recharge their minds and bodies. In fact, without rest, we falter, stumble, and lose effectiveness. Rest, on the other hand, brings renewed productivity, a sharpened mind, and a better attitude. Taking a day off is advantageous to everyone involved.

God knows that tired, restless humans bring stress and angst to others and ultimately far less is accomplished. He invites us to rest not only for our own sake but also to be more effective in our lives and ministries. Some come to their senses the hard way. J. Dana Trent was one of them.

This ordained minister started her Sabbath observance after visiting the doctor's office. The doctor told Trent she needed to "slow down" when he found out she was working four different adjunct jobs and commuting up to two hours per day. She was diagnosed with chronic migraine syndrome. As a result of her own journey, she wrote the book *For Sabbath's Sake: Embracing Your Need for Rest, Worship, and Community*. In it, she writes, "Observing the Sabbath means trusting that if she takes time off, the world won't spin out of control. It's an act of humility that puts God at the center of her life, not herself."[53]

God has never implicitly promised the strength for humans to work without rest at least one day per week. But the good news is that our energy can be restored, refreshed, and then re-harnessed, if we are willing to rest and recharge.

Scheduling Rest

A lot of people have great intentions but lousy priorities. In other words, they want and desire to take a weekly day of rest, but they are not willing to schedule it into their calendars. They live under the mentality that if it happens, it happens, but if it doesn't, it won't. And with this mentality, it usually doesn't happen. Marva J. Dawn writes,

> The key to experiencing the Sabbath in the richness of its design is to recognize the importance of its rhythm. Which day is used to observe the Sabbath is not as important as ensuring that the day of ceasing occurs every seven days without fail.[54]

Notice the phrase "occurs every seven days without fail." Dawn is highlighting an important rhythm that our bodies yearn for.

From the hard-knocks of failure to prioritizing this weekly rhythm—and the resulting burnout, I've come to realize that I desperately need to prioritize my day off. I need to plan when I'll take a day off and then fiercely guard that day against all intrusion.

My wife and I get together at the beginning of each month to place our days off in our calendars. And often it's not easy to find the days that work for each of us. We must think through various options because of travel or other scheduling conflicts. We go back and forth until we both agree.

At times, we've had to schedule our days off separately because of schooling, family events, travel commitments, or other circumstances. I would prefer to take a day off together, but sometimes this is impossible, especially when I'm traveling.

And sometimes the spacing between our days off isn't exactly seven days. We might have to stretch one week to eight or nine days before finding the right day. But if the month has five weeks, we find five days off during that month. Or if it's a four-week month, our goal is to take four different days off during that month.

The goal is to make it habit-forming, to come to the place in which your body knows and can expect that wonderful day of rest—like a horse returning to the water trough after a long ride. Don't mess around with rest. Your body needs it and even craves it.

Guiding Principles for a Day Off

We encouraged a good friend of ours to take a day off. She came back saying, "Okay, so what would a day off look like?" My wife and I explained to her key principles for taking a day off and more specifically, what we do on a day off. We emphasized the need for freedom from legalism and that the principle of rest had more to do with renewal and avoiding stress.

Freedom should guide the day off. The day off should never be controlled by a list of dos and don'ts. I believe the day of rest should be focused on the general theme of relaxing, spending time with family, and loving God. Legalism puts people into a strait-jacket and stifles fun and creativity. There's no one right way to take a day off. In fact, a day off is all about avoiding routine—to not do those things that are considered "work" on the other days of the week.

Each person must define what regular work is versus relaxing and recharging. The idea is to do the interesting things that you can't or don't do during the week. It's removing yourself from stress-related activity and receiving renewal. Granted, we should not neglect the small, necessary house chores, like washing dishes, taking out the trash, and so forth.

Rest

A day off involves relaxing, which means getting a lot of sleep. I have a goal of sleeping seventeen hours between the night before my day off and the night of my day off. That is, I like to average 8.5 hours between those two nights. I'll be talking more about daily sleep in the next chapter, but the day off is a super-charged time to rest, and sleep plays a key part. The psalmist said, "It is in vain that you rise up early and go late to rest, eating the bread of anxious toil; for he gives to his beloved sleep" (Psalm 127:2 ESV).

Yet, more than sleep, a day off is a time of relaxation. The goal is zero stress. I personally believe that the only criteria for an excellent day can be found in the following two questions:

- "Did I fully relax?"
- "Was I able to avoid "normal work" and enjoy God and others?"

I talked to one pastor who differentiated a day off and the Sabbath. He believed that a Sabbath had to be completely spiritual, while a day off was more for rest. Maybe he's right, but I think he was overcomplicating things. Most people cannot commit to both a separate "Sabbath" (spiritual day) and a day of rest and relaxing (day off). And I only see the one day of the 7-day week in Scripture when God asks us to cease from regular work.

Of course, the day off is certainly not a time to avoid spiritual disciplines. However, it's possible to become overly rigid and even legalistic in our thinking that the day off should be entirely dedicated to spirituality. Rather, I think we should live and walk with God spiritually every day of the week. The reality is that the best type of day off is both spiritual and restful. While we should cease from all regular work on a day off, we should also emphasize spirituality and time with God.

I personally like to vary my devotional activity on my day off—focusing on doing spiritual activity that I wouldn't normally do in my daily devotions, like watch a video on God's creation, read a different portion of Scripture, walking and praying, and so forth. Recently, I watched *The Case for Christ* and then rejoiced in what Jesus means to me. On the other six days, my devotional time is very similar, so on my day off, I like to break the mold a bit.

Each person should wrestle with balancing spirituality and fun. But the word *rest* should guide the day off. The day off is the time to renew energy and strength for the long, hard work week ahead.

Enjoyment

We said to our friend, "What brings rest and joy to you?" Do it on your day off. "What is stress-free for you?" Do it. Each person is different in the area of enjoyment. Some find enjoyment in gardening while others would see this as stressful. Some might work on a wood project or art painting. Some enjoy model airplanes, cycling, and so forth. I love watching documentaries, listening to audiobooks, and reading non-work-related books.

More than anything, the day off should break the routine, the molds. I think the phrase in Leviticus is significant when referring to the day off. God told his chosen people, "Do no regular work" (Leviticus 23:24–25). Six days are dedicated to working and getting things done. One day needs to be reoriented to do no regular work—nothing that normally comes under the category of work.

My wife and I have an agreement that we won't talk about things that produce anxiety between us on our days off. Both of us have the prerogative to ask the other not to bring up stress-producing topics, like work-related items, scheduling, emails, and things to do around the house.

I've learned not to read my emails or answer the phone on my day off. Both can wait. Too many times, out of curiosity, I've peeked at an email or answered a phone call that produced anxiety and sapped my peace during my day off. At times, I'll write a quick response saying, "On my day off . . . will call you or write tomorrow."

It's better to forewarn certain people the day before your day off. Some use the automatic reply on their email servers. I do this for my vacations but up until this point have figured that people can wait one day for my reply. And now with WhatsApp, texting, messaging, and calling, it's difficult to cover all bases with a "wait for tomorrow" message.

Emergencies are something entirely different. Again, legalism should be avoided. You might not keep your day off perfectly but remember, there is now no condemnation for those who are in Christ (Romans 8:1). Just remember the principle of rest. The day off is for your benefit.

For example, on my day off, I recently looked at two email subject lines that created stress and frustration. I suddenly found myself worrying about the next day's work. Positively, my wife received a scheduling change that involved me, but she was gracious to simply say that we would talk about it the next day (we've learned from failure and experience to do this).

The words of Christ should be applied to our day off, "Therefore do not worry about tomorrow, for tomorrow will worry about itself. Each day has enough trouble of its own" (Matthew 6:34). While this applies to every day of the week, it should be the motto of the day off. One day should be completely stress-free, relaxed, peaceful, and full of rest.

Taking a regular day off won't necessarily happen right away. But as you work at it, taking a day of rest will become a habit. First, make it a conviction and eventually, it will also become a habit. Victory follows.

Family

When my family was young, we would spend our day off finding interesting things to do around Southern California. We consulted a book of places to visit which we referred to as the "yellow book." The author had personally gone to most of the places with her family and then wrote a book about her experiences. We tried most of the author's suggestions.

In the evening, we would watch a favorite movie together, order food, and just hang out. Rest and relaxation were the focus.

Nowadays, our kids are older and out of the house, so our day off is different. Celyce likes to sit out in the backyard and have her quiet time, read a novel, and just relax. I love documentaries, audiobooks, and non-fiction books that have nothing to do with my own ministry. I just want to *space out*. Then we come together in the afternoon to pray, walk, and watch something together. We often go out to eat or bring something home. We have read a book together or listened to an audiobook. Our goal is enjoyment and rest.

Extended Rest: Vacations

The principle of rest starts with a day off, but it shouldn't stop there. Rest should also include extended vacation time as well.

In the Old Testament, we often see annual festivals in which God provided extended rest and recreation (Leviticus 23). The God who loves rest wanted his people to seek him and do no work for even longer periods. For seven days, they were not to do any regular work.

Our bodies need extended rest, and that's what vacation time is all about. On various occasions, I've heard people boast that they work all year and never take vacations. Some have even boasted of never taking a vacation in their entire lives. This is a sad commentary and certainly not impressive. I've been growing in my understanding and commitment to yearly vacations.

Chuck Bentley, chief executive officer for Crown Financial Ministries, gives several important, common sense reasons why longer vacations are necessary:

- The brain functions better after rest.
- When the mind and body relax, overall health boosts.
- Creativity, productivity, and quality of work improve after vacations.
- Episodes of depression diminish.
- Sleep improves.
- Our souls are restored.
- We gain greater appreciation for nature and people of diverse cultures.
- Goal achievement is enhanced.
- Families are strengthened.
- Sense of balance is renewed when the rhythm of work and rest is reset.
- Burnouts are prevented.[55]

Will Maule notes, "Recent studies show that American workers are far more productive after returning from a vacation, because of the fact that increased hours of sleep and decreased levels of stress (direct results of vacation) led to more productivity."[56]

Some people take an entire month off. Others take two-weeks. A lot depends on company policy, among other things. We've decided to take three weeks off per year. We are self-employed and have more liberty in this area. Yet, it would be easy to work fifty-two weeks out of the year. So we've decided on at least three weeks of total rest.

I'm an achiever and could easily fall into the trap of not taking vacation time, but I've grown in my understanding of the discipline of rest and the need to commit myself to take my vacations. Like our day-off planning, my wife and I map out our three weeks together and make sure we include those times in the calendar.

In the past, I would try to sneak in emails and other work during my vacation time when my family was sleeping or wasn't noticing. Later, I was coaching another pastor who ended up coaching me. He had just come back from a lovely time with his family and naturally shared that he didn't do any work on his vacations. I listened and stammered out a few encouraging words, but I realized that God was speaking to me about ceasing from work and just resting.

In 2019, I spoke on rest and vacations in West New York, New Jersey, and a business owner came up to me afterward, thanking me profusely. He had concluded that he should cancel his annual vacation time in order to give more time to his business. But God spoke to him that morning. He concluded that refreshing his family was the most important business in life and that God would bless his business as a result. His wife was thrilled by his decision that day.

The Marathon

The Christian life is a marathon, not a fifty-yard dash. God has called us to live well for a long period of time on this earth. Granted, he will call some home earlier than others, but let's make sure that our departure isn't premature because of the lack of rest.

Recently, a friend in his early fifties had a heart attack. This person worked day and night and ignored the calls of his body to rest. He was the first to volunteer at the church, and I often heard him say, "I can't refuse the Lord's work."

God wants us to prioritize rest. As we commit ourselves to taking one day off per week, as well as extended vacations, we will become more fruitful and live in greater victory. The God of rest asks us to do this, and he knows what's best for us.

Points to Consider

- What is the main principle you've learned from this chapter? How will you apply it?
- What is hindering you from taking one day of rest each week?
- What steps do you need to take to prioritize one day of rest? Vacations?
- What will you do differently on your day of rest after reading this chapter?

.

Spiritual Truth #7

Care for Your Body

Joan came up for prayer after church one Sunday morning, sharing how she wasn't experiencing God's presence in her life. The pastor invited her out for coffee and listened to her story.

It soon became apparent that Joan worked sixty-five hours per week, primarily ate junk food, did not exercise, and slept little. She had to leave the meeting to get back to the office. She wanted a magical cure, but the pastor knew that wasn't going to happen. Why? Because she was not ready for change. She wasn't willing to take care of her body, exercise sufficiently, and get more sleep.

A few months later, she hit a wall physically and had to be hospitalized for depression that came about through her sheer exhaustion. The pastor met her soon afterward and talked to her about taking care of her body. She was finally willing to hear him.

While most are not as extreme as Joan, many people today are experiencing life in similar ways to Joan. They are living and working but not taking care of themselves. They are also experiencing little victory.

The good news is that Joan began to take responsibility for her physical condition. She learned the hard way that her physical health directly affected her mental, emotional, and spiritual life. Joan is a different person today. She's experiencing more victory and confidence in her Christian life.

The Body Myth

Many believe that the way they treat their bodies has no bearing on their walk with God. They do not exercise regularly or eat healthy food. Nor is it a priority. Spirituality, yes; physical health, no. They subtly have placed a wall between the two.

They are offended when pastors and leaders bring up healthy living. After all, isn't this a private matter? Why waste time talking about physical health? "After all, the body will soon perish and our spirits will remain forever," they say. People are open to hearing about spiritual and eternal principles but not about the proper care of their bodies.

Gnosticism, a major philosophy during New Testament times, taught that the body was bad and that the spiritual was good. Gnostics distinguished between the physical realm, which was evil, and the spiritual or enlightened sphere, which could only be understood by a special *gnosis,* which means secret or spiritual knowledge. And, of course, only the Gnostics could provide this special knowledge.

Although we wouldn't call it Gnosticism today, the same separation of the body and the spirit exists among those who only focus on the soul, while forgetting the body—a sort of Christian Gnosticism. The reality, however, is that God does care for our bodies, and we are able to experience far more victory when our bodies are healthy.

God Designed the Body

The book of Genesis tells us that God created us in his image (Genesis 1:27). Humans are the only creatures who are spiritual, rational, emotional, and can make clear choices, like being able to serve the Creator or reject him. Irenaeus, an influential early church father, emphasized the body as an essential aspect of the image of God, citing the incarnation of Jesus Christ.[57]

When Jesus Christ came down to this earth to redeem his creation, he came in a human body—not a disembodied spirit but as a human being with a physical body. John says, "The Word became flesh" (John 1:14). After his death and before he ascended into heaven, the disciples recognized his scars (John 20:27). And even in his exalted state today, Christ's body is still recognizable (Revelation 21:3–4; 22:4). He will forever be the God-Man who sacrificed himself for us.

The gospel claims that as believers our bodies—not just our souls—are united to the living Christ. We are physical extensions of Christ in the modern world. Paul says,

> Do you not know that your bodies are members of Christ himself? Shall I then take the members of Christ and unite them with a prostitute? Never! Do you not know that he who unites himself with a prostitute is one with her in body? For it is said, "The two will become one flesh." But whoever is united with the Lord is one with him in spirit. Flee from sexual immorality. All other sins a person commits are outside the body, but whoever sins sexually, sins against their own body. Do you not know that your bodies are temples of the Holy Spirit, who is in you, whom you have received from God? You are not your own; you were bought at a price. Therefore honor God with your bodies. (1 Corinthians 6:15–20)

These verses clearly teach that our bodies are God's temple. The context of 1 Corinthians 6 is prostitution and the need to abstain from uniting the body with a prostitute. Why? Because the body is God's holy temple and such activity is demeaning to the God who lives inside. John Piper, well-known author and speaker, wrote about why he avoided smoking cigarettes while growing up,

> My mother's statement, "Son, your body is the temple of the Holy Ghost, and giving yourself lung cancer for that kind of pleasure would not treat the Holy Spirit rightly." That worked for me! Still does.[58]

The question, "What would Jesus do?" applies to decisions about our bodies. As we walk around, we are carrying the Trinity. He lives within us. Scripture tells us that God was in Christ reconciling the world to himself (2 Corinthians 5:19), and in a very similar way, God walks around in us. Christians are to glorify God in our bodies because our bodies are temples of the Holy Spirit. Proper care of the bodies God has given us is important in achieving victorious living.

Paul's prayer for the Thessalonians included proper care of the body. He writes, "May God himself, the God of peace, sanctify you through and through. May your whole spirit, soul and body be kept blameless at the coming of our Lord Jesus Christ" (1 Thessalonians 5:23). For Paul, the body had an important place in living a victorious, holy lifestyle.

Self-Control, the Fruit of the Spirit

When writing to the Corinthians, Paul mimicked their common slogan, "You say, 'Food for the stomach and the stomach for food, and God will destroy them both'" (1 Corinthians 6:13). Many in Corinth acted like it didn't matter what they ate or how much they ate. Notice Paul's response, "'I have the right to do anything,' you say—but not everything is beneficial. 'I have the right to do anything'—but I will not be mastered by anything" (1 Corinthians 6:12). Paul continues with an exhortation on self-control and avoidance of sinful bodily appetites in order to honor God with the body.

In Galatians 5:23, one manifestation of the fruit of the Holy Spirit is self-control (Galatians 5:23). Christians are to exhibit self-control in all areas of life, including eating and physical activity. Many, however, make an exception for self-control in the area of physical health. Jeremy Bell, lead pastor at New Hope Baptist Church in Greenville, South Carolina, writes,

How can we exhort people to have self-control in spiritual matters when we stand in front of them overweight, out of shape and with no self-control in physical matters? Additionally, if you are a good steward of your body, your physical health will give you more energy and endurance to . . . share Christ with your neighbors.[59]

God has called us to be good stewards of our bodies. As stewards. we have a responsibility before God and others to take care of our bodies.

I have a good friend who is a head nurse in an urgent care facility in Washington. He sees patients all the time who check into urgent care due to excess eating, drinking, unhealthy eating, and so forth. He told me that people often think that their bodies are their own and that they can do anything they want with them. But he has seen firsthand how selfish this is. Why? Because a person's health immediately affects those closest to them. The husbands, wives, children, family members, and friends are the ones who nurse the patient back to health, visit them in the hospital, and generally sacrifice because of the poor choices their loved ones have made.

We should allow the Holy Spirit to fill us and give us the self-control to take good care of our bodies. We need to maintain self-control by eating healthy foods, exercising, and getting enough sleep. We should resist anything that controls us, whether sexual sins, gluttony, or any other addictive bad habits.

Maximizing Your Body's Health

My ninety-four-old mother is very healthy. She gets plenty of sleep, eats healthy foods, and regularly exercises. Her good health allows her to visit neighbors and friends. God continues to use her, and a key reason for her victory is because she has done a great job of taking care of herself.

Yet, my mother, like everyone else, will eventually pass away. Everyone will die, usually because of a physical affliction, whether from cancer, heart attack, or other illness. Thankfully, God has given us doctors and hospitals to diagnose problems and offer remedies. We should take advantage of them. It's preferable, however, to avoid the hospital altogether through preventative, healthy living.

Many people, like those who survive a heart attack, speak glowingly afterward about healthy eating, sleeping, and proper exercise. Hindsight is so much clearer than foresight. My friend Jeff Tunnel suffered a full cardiac arrest and was in a coma for four days. Before his heart attack, Jeff had little conviction about the food he ate. But after his heart attack, Jeff became a new man. He became extremely diligent about only eating certain foods and avoiding everything else. Jeff is doing better than ever today, serving Jesus with new vitality and is committed to healthy eating.

When our bodies are sluggish, tired, and unhealthy, all that we do for Jesus is hindered. On the other hand, healthy bodies are more effective in fulfilling God's plan and purpose. When we're healthy, we have more energy to do God's work. We need to be willing to allow God to change us and give us the discipline to make those choices that empower and revitalize our bodies.

Getting Enough Sleep

Sometimes we think there's a spiritual answer for everything, and we ignore the physical. But often our discouragement, irritations, and impatience have more to do with our physical or mental conditions.

Elijah faced this dilemma when running from Jezebel after calling down fire and killing the 400 prophets of Baal. He had trusted God to do amazing things and God had answered. With God's help, he single-handedly defeated 400 false prophets. But he was also exhausted.

Then he received a threat from Jezebel, his archrival, that tipped the scale emotionally. We read, "So Jezebel sent a messenger to Elijah to say, 'May the gods deal with me, be it ever so severely, if by this time tomorrow I do not make your life like that of one of them'" (1 Kings 19:2). Elijah's response? We read, "Elijah was afraid and ran for his life" (1 Kings 19:3).

How could this man of God become so afraid of one leader? The answer is exhaustion. We see the importance of not being severely exhausted in the way God treated Elijah on his journey to Horeb. God made sure Elijah slept and ate before arriving at the destination. Scripture says,

> Then he lay down under the bush and fell asleep. All at once an angel touched him and said, "Get up and eat." He looked around, and there by his head was some bread baked over hot coals, and a jar of water. He ate and drank and then lay down again. The angel of the LORD came back a second time and touched him and said, "Get up and eat, for the journey is too much for you." So he got up and ate and drank. (1 Kings 19:5–8)

When we're exhausted or in poor health, it becomes difficult to accomplish anything. What might appear to be a spiritual dilemma, really has physical roots. We often forget that we are physical, mental, and emotional beings.

We do everything better with enough sleep. Experts say that a normal person needs about seven hours of sleep per night. For some, that might be too little.[60] Our bodies just work better when rested. Sleep renews us and contributes to our vitality and vibrancy. Sleep repairs the body and gets us ready for the next day.

I've learned this truth the hard way. On many occasions, my lack of sleep caused increased irritation, faulty decisions, and discouragement. One week in October 2019, I was preparing to coach pastors and leaders, but I had not been sleeping well during the week. And this was also after weeks of busy travel. I had booked my days full of coaching leaders without the proper nightly sleep.

On one of my calls, I felt oppressed, heavy, and discouraged. I could barely talk with the leader I was coaching. I went away thinking, "Lord, what happened? Was Satan attacking me? Had I lost the joy of coaching leaders? I spent time worshipping and pleading for God's grace. And yes, this helped but it didn't solve the problem. I pressed through the rest of my coaching calls and went to bed, hoping that during my morning devotions, God would show me what went wrong.

The answer came loud and clear: I was simply wiped out, too tired. The dark, blackness that accompanied the previous day's phone call was the result of exhaustion. Even though I had been taking my regular days off, I failed to get enough daily sleep. I simply didn't have enough physical strength to keep pressing on. My body was resisting me. More sleep was my answer.

Before taking the rest of the coaching calls, I got some sleep and made sure I received plenty of extra rest which resulted in my feeling strong and confident in my coaching. I had new energy, life, direction, and joy.

Bodily health affects all we say and do. If we're worn out, it's going to show. If we feel sick, we'll accomplish little. A body dragged down by lack of sleep, unhealthy eating, and lack of exercise won't function very well and might even cause us to manifest anger, impatience, and depression.

Eating Well

In 2018, I spoke at twenty-four conferences in many different countries and contexts. I practiced the missionary creed of eating everything on my plate. But I also suffered for it. I was overweight, my cholesterol was elevated, and I had to go to the emergency room three times because of a tear duct problem, which eventually required surgery. I frequently felt tired. While trying to give to others, I often felt like someone needed to be pouring into my own life.

By the end of the year, I was sick, bloated, and out of shape.[61] I turned to my wife on a plane ride from Washington to Los Angeles in December 2018, saying, "Help me." I showed her a picture I had taken at a Methodist conference in Brazil a few months earlier, which showed my waistline bulging from the conference t-shirt. "I need help," I pleaded.

In January 2019, I made some key changes. I decided to follow a strict, plant-based diet. I lost twenty pounds and have kept those pounds off. I now only eat three meals per day, avoid snacks, and focus on eating particular foods (e.g., vegetables, salads, fruits, beans, etc.).[62]

As I write, I can confidently say that in the last year and a half, I've had far more energy and have accomplished more for Jesus and others. When I'm relating to family, coaching pastors, speaking at a conference, writing books, or ministering in my local church, I feel a renewed vitality and vibrancy. I have far more victory now than before. A lot of the dullness has disappeared, and I'm able to give myself more fully to God and his work. I've discovered afresh that health is critical to everything I do.

Many great books on healthy eating have appeared in the last ten years. Joel Fuhrman's *Eat to Live* is one of my favorites.[63] T. Colin Campbell's *The China Study* and Michael Greger's *Do Not Die* are also excellent. I also highly recommend Dr. McDougal's books and his free newsletter and articles. John A. McDougall is an American physician and author who founded Right Foods Inc.

These books, and many like them, view weight loss as a byproduct of healthy eating, not the main focus. Dieting, in fact, rarely works. Studies have proven that weight taken off through diets comes right back. At the same time, some food not only nourishes the body but helps a person lose weight (e.g., fruits, vegetables, salad, etc.). The packaged, man-made variety of foods, on the other hand, are mostly harmful and add excess weight.

Many use the *Daniel Fast* as a short-term focus on vegetables and water for typically three weeks in order to draw closer to God as well as to cleanse the body of toxins. The fast is based on the diet of Daniel in chapter 1, where the Scriptures record that he ate vegetables for ten days. However, there is an eating plan inspired by Daniel's fast that is designed to encourage more lasting change. Pastor Rick Warren created *The Daniel Plan* after realizing he and his congregants needed to lose weight.

The reality is that most writing on the topic of healthy eating says the same thing: avoid dairy, processed foods, and meats. Focus on salads, vegetables, legumes, and fruit.

The food we eat makes a huge impact on how we function. It can make the difference between living in victory or not. The nutrients in food enable the cells in our bodies to work properly. Food nutrients are essential for the growth, development, and maintenance of our body functions. Many studies over a long time period have confirmed that the types of food we eat make a huge difference on how our bodies function. Eating healthy fine-tunes our bodies and gives us strength and vitality to better serve God.

Exercise

Paul said to Timothy, "For physical training is of some value, but godliness has value for all things, holding promise for both the present life and the life to come" (1 Timothy 4:8). Paul tells us that exercise does have value and that godliness should also be considered a high value for Christians who desire to be faithful followers.

Exercising regularly is essential for optimal health. God has made the body to exercise, to move around. The term *couch potato* describes a person who spends little or no time exercising and a great deal of time watching television. Couch potatoes sit at work, sit in their car, and then sit while watching TV. This combination of sitting and not exercising increases the risk of dying by 37 percent, according to a study of 123,216 people who were followed over a fourteen-year period.[64]

Any exercise is better than none. Granted, the best type of exercise is strenuous enough to get the blood pumping to strengthen the heart, which includes walking, running, jogging, dancing, swimming, and just about anything that keeps the body moving. Paige Waehner, a personal trainer, writes:

> If you hate gym workouts, don't force yourself onto a treadmill. Walk, jog, or bike outdoors to enjoy the scenery. If you like socializing, consider sports, group fitness, working out with a friend or a walking club. Choose something you can see yourself doing at least three days a week. To meet the exercise recommendations, you need to do cardio three days per week. Make it easier to be motivated by choosing an activity that will be convenient for you to do that often, at least until you've formed the habit.[65]

Running was my exercise of choice for most of my life. I ran consistently for several miles in the morning. I even trained for and completed a half-marathon. Then I developed a "runner's hernia" (Inguinal hernia) in 2011. The doctor who operated suggested that I trade in my running for walking. I took his advice.

Since 2011, my goal is walking 14,000 steps per day, and I usually come close to fulfilling this. When I exercise, my mind is more in tune, and I can accomplish much more for his glory. Just the opposite occurs when I sit for long periods without walking.

Most people, however, don't need to average 14,000 steps per day. One Harvard study of nearly 17,000 women concluded that those who walked 7,500 steps or more had the lowest mortality rate. Even women who walked 4,400 steps had a lower mortality rate than those who were the least active and walked only about 2,000 steps.[66]

Some people find trainers to guide them in the exercise process. I commend this type of commitment and all those who exercise regularly and seriously. The key is getting off the couch and getting the body moving.

While we're on this earth and in a physical body, God desires that we keep it as healthy as possible. We can live far more victoriously when our bodies are alert, vibrant, and responding to the Holy Spirit's direction.

Measure How You're Doing

"If you want something to count in your life, it helps to figure out a way to count it."[67] This commonsense quote applies to sports, business, or personal life goals. It also applies to good health. I've found it very helpful to measure my sleep, exercise, and eating each week. I do better at fulfilling my goals if I'm measuring them. Each day, I write down the number of steps I've taken, hours I've slept, and whether I ate healthy food (if you'd like to see how I measure my own progress, please see the Appendix).

Measurable progress in achieving and maintaining personal goals regarding eating, exercise, and sleep is essential. A person will unlikely achieve and maintain their required amount of sleep, exercise, and a proper diet for a healthy lifestyle without some measurable form of accounting so they can see their progress and make adjustments. All measurements need to be done under grace, not legalism, with understanding that a healthy lifestyle is beneficial to victorious living. Only the cross of Jesus makes us whole, not healthy eating, adequate exercising, or getting enough sleep. Grace needs to cover all our efforts, or we end up becoming self-righteous and judgmental.

Not Your Own

All people are created in the image of God and are valuable to the Creator. Believers in Christ have been redeemed by the blood of Jesus Christ, and our lives belong to him. For this reason, we should honor God in all aspects of our lives, and this includes taking care of our bodies.

The spiritual and emotional aspects of life are essential but the physical side is critical and often overlooked in the quest for a victorious lifestyle. Regular exercise, sleep, and eating a healthy diet optimizes health and helps us to live a more fruitful life. Rest is essential to victorious living, so is proper nutrition, exercise, and getting enough sleep.

And the good news is that soon we will be changed and given new heavenly bodies. Paul gives us a glimpse of this when he says, "Listen, I tell you a mystery: We will not all sleep, but we will all be changed— in a flash, in the twinkling of an eye, at the last trumpet. For the trumpet will sound, the dead will be raised imperishable, and we will be changed. For the perishable must clothe itself with the imperishable, and the mortal with immortality. When the perishable has been clothed with the imperishable, and the mortal with immortality, then the saying that is written will come true: 'Death has been swallowed up in victory'" (1 Corinthians 15:51–54).

Points to Consider

- What is the main principle you've learned from this chapter? How will you apply it?

- On a scale of 1–10, how would you rate your eating habits? Exercise? Sleep?

- Between sleep, healthy eating, and exercise, what do you need to work on most?

- What can you do to improve in each of these areas?

Keep the End in View

Only one life 'twill soon be past.
Only what's done for Christ will last.

C. T. Studd, the author of the poem, "Only One Life, 'Twill Soon Be Past," abandoned his fame and fortune to become a missionary on three continents.

C. T. Studd was a famous cricket player at Trinity College in Cambridge in 1883. When his brother, George, became seriously ill, he was confronted by the question, "What is all the fame and flattery worth when a man comes to face eternity?"[68] C. T. Studd changed completely. He wrote at the time, "I know that cricket would not last, and honor would not last, and nothing in this world would last, but it was worthwhile living for the world to come."[69] When he received his father's inheritance, he gave it all away to missions.

He went to China in February 1885 along with six others. They served with Hudson Taylor at the China Inland Mission. While in China, C. T. Studd wrote, "Some want to live within the sound of church or chapel bell; I want to run a rescue shop within a yard of hell."

From China, C. T. Studd and his young family went to India, where between 1900–1906, they served as missionary pastors. While back in England due to poor health, he was intrigued by a notice saying, "Cannibals want missionaries." Dr. Karl Kumm, a German explorer, passionately presented the need to preach the gospel in Africa among the tribes who had never heard the Good

News. Studd answered God's call and spent the next twenty-one years ministering in the unreached Congo region of Africa.

In total, he had spent some fifteen years in China, six in India, and twenty-one years spreading the Gospel in Africa.

At the age of nineteen, God called me to be a missionary after reading Norman Grubb's *C. T. Studd: Cricketeer & Pioneer.* Through C. T. Studd's example, I became increasingly aware of the shortness of this life compared to the immensity of eternity. I left California with the goal of joining WEC international, the organization that Studd founded. I eventually became a missionary with The Christian and Missionary Alliance, but C. T. Studd's example stirred me to begin the missionary process.

C.T. Studd is not alone in prioritizing the next life. The heroes in Hebrews 11 had their minds set on the end game. They realized their true victory was in heaven. Scripture tells us:

> . . . who through faith, conquered kingdoms, administered justice, and gained what was promised; who shut the mouths of lions, quenched the fury of the flames, and escaped the edge of the sword; whose weakness was turned to strength; and who became powerful in battle and routed foreign armies. Women received back their dead, raised to life again. There were others who were tortured, refusing to be released so that they might gain an even better resurrection. (Hebrews 11:33–35)

The phrase "that they might gain an even better resurrection" drove them and stirred them onward. They were motivated by the resurrection and eternal priorities.

Hurry Up and Enjoy

People realize that life is short and that death comes quickly. But their solution is to get as much out of this short life as possible. We see this in many advertising campaigns:

- "Grab for all the pleasure you can. Right now."

- "Get your mind out of the clouds and live in the here and now."
- "Prosper."
- "Make your mark now."

I live in southern California—the land of Hollywood tinsel and stardom. It's not uncommon to read in the *Los Angeles Times* about a movie star buying a mansion sitting on hundreds of acres of prime real estate. The article will describe the incredible view, dozens of rooms, and all the other perks. The readers are supposed to be impressed—and envious—because of the luxurious palace that everyone should want or dream about.

The reality is that enjoyment in this life is short-lived and living for now is short-sighted. I, like many, enjoyed visiting the pyramids of Egypt as a tourist. I was impressed by the monuments of time but saddened by the mistaken belief that kings and queens could take physical possessions with them to the next life. The loaded treasure in the pyramids stands as a reminder of the folly of trying to transport things from this earth to the next one.

Ultimate victory comes through keeping the end in view and focusing on the next life.

Realize Life Is Short

A doctor friend who specializes in cancer told me about people's reactions when she breaks the sad news to them that they only have a few weeks or months to live. Some of them rebel and demand more time. They can't believe that their lives will soon end. They might challenge her diagnosis and demand new information. They beg her for other interpretations, new remedies, and additional information. In other words, they can't believe that their lives are hanging in the balance and that they're facing an uncertain future. But for most of them, she told me, there is little medical science can do.

The reality is that all of us are only here on this earth for a short time. James says, "Now listen, you who say, 'Today or tomorrow we will go to this or that city, spend a year there, carry on business and make money.' Why, you do not even know what will happen tomorrow. What is your life? You are a mist that appears for a little while and then vanishes. Instead, you ought to say, "If it is the Lord's will, we will live and do this or that" (James 4:13–15). Time is fleeting. The good news for Christians is that true victory is in the next life.

Jesus, knowing the reality of eternity, said, "Watch out! Be on your guard against all kinds of greed; life does not consist in an abundance of possessions" (Luke 12:15). He gave a parable of a certain rich man who yielded an abundant harvest.

> He thought to himself, "What shall I do? I have no place to store my crops." "Then he said, 'This is what I'll do. I will tear down my barns and build bigger ones, and there I will store my surplus grain. And I'll say to myself, 'You have plenty of grain laid up for many years. Take life easy; eat, drink and be merry.' "But God said to him, 'You fool! This very night your life will be demanded from you. Then who will get what you have prepared for yourself?' "This is how it will be with whoever stores up things for themselves but is not rich toward God." (Luke 12:17-21)

Life is so short, and as believers, we will soon be with Jesus. True wisdom tells us not to hold on to earth's possessions and to be aware that we could pass away at any time.

In 2009, I gave a seminar in Monterrey, Mexico, at an Assembly of God church, pastored by Noe Salinas. I figured this would be another *normal* seminar. Various leaders gathered to share the vision for world missions in the city of Monterrey.

We sat around Noe's long table for lunch and dinner, sharing stories and memories of our lives and ministry. His wife showered us with hospitality, and Noe even invited family members to join us, along with his youth pastor and wife, who were excited about missions and where the church was going.

After the conference, Noe, along with his youth pastor, showed me his small group offices, pointing out how he planned on expanding his small group outreach to include new sectors of the city. *I look forward to hearing about this church a lot in the future,* I thought. I liked his plain, simple style and felt excited about where the church was headed.

We said our goodbyes and left. Within two months of our visit, Noe and his youth pastor were dead. Gone from this earth. Welcomed into eternity.

Their deaths happened unexpectantly, but the cause of their deaths could have happened to anyone in the room. Noe died of a heart attack and the youth pastor died of another physical ailment.

Noe was probably fifty-five years old and the youth pastor might have been twenty-five. They both left behind families. God was pleased to take them earlier than the rest of us, like Enoch in Genesis 5, who was transported suddenly from one life to the next.

Both pastor Noe and his youth pastor were ready for eternity. They were living for Jesus and ready to go. They lived in victory in this life and are now rejoicing in their new inheritance, their new bodies, and all that God has for them. Paul said, "For to me, to live is Christ and to die is gain" (Philippians 1:21).

We will be there soon. Each day is a gift from God that we need to treasure. Linda Stangl, a godly friend and leader at the Journey Church in Big Bear, California, often sat in my living room with her husband Joe. Linda, an elder for many years at the Journey Church, accompanied Pastor Jeff Tunnel to learn about small groups. In September 2016, Jeff Tunnel survived a full cardiac arrest and Linda and I met each other at the hospital while visiting him.

Only a few months later, Linda was notified that she had cancer. She lived one week after she received the news. She didn't even know she was sick, but in one week, she was in the presence of Jesus. Linda trusted the Holy Spirit and clung to him throughout her life, including those final days.

Prepare for an Extraordinary Future

Stephen Covey, in his bestselling book, *The 7 Habits of Highly Effective People,* counsels people to envision what they desire people to say at their funeral and then start working backward to fulfill those expectations. Covey wisely tells people to start with the end in view and allow that endgame to play out in the here and now. Covey knows that when a person is constantly envisioning the endgame, he or she can better prioritize those things that are important right now, knowing the end will come soon.

I like Covey's counsel, but I don't think it goes far enough. I don't get overly motivated thinking about what people might say at my funeral. I suppose all of us would love to have nice things said at our funerals, but we'll be dead, so we won't be able to enjoy them. And the reality is that people are supposed to say nice things at funerals.

So what should we be envisioning? I think we should be envisioning what Jesus will say to us when we enter his presence. After all, what he thinks and says at that time is far more important than what people think or say about us in the here and now. Jesus knows everything. People don't see the thoughts and intentions of our heart. And what Jesus thinks will have eternal consequences. I personally long for him to say, "Well done, good and faithful servant!" (Matthew 25:23). I then want to live right now so those words will become a reality.

Christians believe they will immediately be in the presence of God after death, Paul said, "I am torn between the two: I desire to depart and be with Christ, which is better by far; but it is more necessary for you that I remain in the body. Convinced of this, I know that I will remain, and I will continue with all of you for your progress and joy in the faith" (Philippians 1:23–25). Scripture says that believers will be rewarded for eternity (1 Corinthians 3:12–15). Those who know him will not only stand before him and live with him, but they will also reap the fruit of their actions for eternity.

I find myself very motivated by that reality. All other opinions matter little. We should be envisioning the joy and beauty of the next life. After all, Scripture says that Jesus is preparing a place for us (John 14:2). I often tell people in my sermons to envision becoming rich in heaven through serving Jesus, rather than only focusing on bigger bank accounts down here. Jesus tells us to lay up our wealth in heaven and not on earth (Matthew 6:19–21). And the good news is that we can store up treasure in heaven by allowing God to produce good works through us.

Revelation tells us that heaven will be free from sickness and curses and that God himself will be the light. We read, "He will wipe every tear from their eyes. There will be no more death or mourning or crying or pain, for the old order of things has passed away" (Revelation 21:4). We will have new bodies. Paul said, "When the perishable has been clothed with the imperishable, and the mortal with immortality, then the saying that is written will come true: 'Death has been swallowed up in victory'" (1 Corinthians 15:54). And most importantly, we'll see Jesus, who has been praying for us continually (Hebrews 7:25).

In his book, *Heaven,* Randy Alcorn writes, "Most people live unprepared for death. But those who are wise will go to a reliable source to investigate what's on the other side. And if they discover that the choices they make during their brief stay in this world will matter in the world to come, they'll want to adjust those choices accordingly."[70] The late pastor Chuck Smith, founder of the Calvary Chapel movement, would often say, "In this life, we are preparing for the next one."

Life on earth is the preparation ground for the eternity that awaits. We must not cling to the things of this world, knowing that we can't take any of it with us. Paul said, "For we brought nothing into the world, and we can take nothing out of it" (1 Timothy 6:7). We are strangers passing through this earth, and we must not think that we will be here for a long time. We won't.

I have a little exercise in my devotions in which I scroll back on my computer calendar to May 06, 1956, the day I was born. I then zoom through all the months and years that have passed, right up to the present time and beyond until I'm 85, on May 06, 2041. The calendar flies by me so quickly and I realize that all the fears and worries of the past are gone and out of mind.

My plans for the future are in God's hands, but I can be sure of one thing: time will pass quickly. Will Jesus come before then? There's a good possibility. But even if he chooses to wait longer for more to be saved, I know my life on this earth will soon be over. This exercise helps me remember that my life is a vapor and that my fears and worries will soon be over and my hopes and dreams will be completely fulfilled.

Chrysostom, an early church father, practiced this type of upward/downward living. He wrote, "Let us then imagine it to be present now [Christ's judgment seat], and reckon each one of us with his own conscience, and account the Judge to be already present, and everything to be revealed and brought forth."[71] This early church father knew that in this life, we need to live as though we could be present before the God of the universe at any moment.

Heavenly Minds Create Earthly Good

One common but untrue criticism of believers is that they are so heavenly minded that they are no earthly good. But the reality is that having an eternal perspective inspires believers to do a lot of earthly good here and now. John Blanchard writes, "Over the centuries, no identifiable group of human beings has had a more positive impact on this world than that comprised of those with a firm belief in the world to come and in the very promises dismissed by humanists as 'illusory and harmful.'"[72] When we live for eternity, we have far more victory in this life as well.

John Stott traces the way in which Christians founded schools, hospitals, and refuges for the outcast. Stott then says, "Later still they abolished the slave trade and freed the slaves, and they improved the conditions of workers in mills and mines and of prisoners in gaols [this is a British term for jails]. They protected children from commercial exploitation in the factories of the West and from ritual prostitution in the temples of the East."[73]

When a person is accountable to the God of the universe to whom they will give account, there's a much greater motivation to help and serve others, in comparison with those who believe life is accidental with no true purpose or direction. Jesus tells us that we will be rewarded for our works here on this earth.

When we are heavenly minded (thinking about the end game), we are actually more earthly good. We know that our loving, gracious God will ask us to give an account on whether we allow him to bear fruit through us and operate his grace in our lives. We'll ultimately give him all the glory for what he has produced in us.

Jesus and the New Testament writers taught that we should be heavenly minded and that we need to constantly remind ourselves that what we do on this earth will have heavenly consequences. Paul told believers to set their minds on things above and not on earthly things (Colossians 3:1-2).

Elisabeth Elliot, wrote the book *Through Gates of Splendor* to describe the five missionaries who laid down their lives for the Auca Indians in the jungles of Ecuador. Jim Elliot, Elisabeth's husband, led the team to Shell Mera, deep in the jungles of Ecuador. Jim coined the saying, "He is no fool who gives what he cannot keep to gain that which he cannot lose." By attempting to reach the Aucas, and ultimately giving up their lives, they inspired countless others to live for eternity.

While living in Ecuador, I took the opportunity to visit the beach where the five missionaries died. While there, I picked up a stone from the beach where they died, and that stone continually reminds me to live for eternity, "He is no fool who gives what he cannot keep to gain that which he cannot lose." Now the entire

Auca tribe is converted and sending missionaries to other tribes. Elliot's work continues to this day. Living for the next life stirs us to live more fully today.

Dietrich Bonhoeffer was living a comfortable life in the U.S. but knew he needed to go back to Germany and suffer with the people of God under Hitler's oppressive policies. He wrote, "God lets himself be pushed out of the world on to the cross . . . The Bible directs man to God's powerlessness and suffering; only the suffering God can help."[74]

Bonhoeffer understood that his true victory was beyond the here and now. He was able to help the suffering church and even attempt to overthrow Hitler because he understood eternal priorities.

Hold on to the Prize

The biblical writers often talked about staying firm to the end. Paul told us to press on to win the prize of the high calling in Christ Jesus (Philippians 3:14). The Christian life is a journey, a battle, and a lifestyle. We are called to hold firm until the end.

Sadly, some walk away midstream. Paul said, "Demas, because he loved this world, has deserted me and has gone to Thessalonica" (2 Timothy 4:10). Falling away from Jesus occurred in Paul's time and it happens today. Trusting in Christ is one thing. Being faithful to the end is another.

I recently talked to Ralph Neighbour Jr., church planter and prolific author. He's now ninety-one. I asked him some general questions, but he got right to the point. "Joel, I just want to go home. I look forward to being with Jesus."

I said to him, "Ralph, if I live to ninety-one, I want to be just like you. You've lived your life for Jesus and served him faithfully to the very end."

God promises his daily grace if we abide in him (John 15:1-4). He wants to fill us daily with his Spirit (Ephesians 5:18). Jude says, "But you, dear friends, by building yourselves up in your most holy faith and praying in the Holy Spirit, keep yourselves in God's love as you wait for the mercy of our Lord Jesus Christ to bring you to eternal life. " (Jude 20–21).

We will soon be with Jesus for eternity. Ask him to give you the strength to hold firm until the end. We need God's daily grace and strength to overcome the challenges that confront us. Knowing that our true home is in heaven, we must place our treasures and resources there. True victory awaits us.

Points to Consider

- What is the main principle you've learned from this chapter? How will you apply it?

- In what areas of your life have you been living for self rather than God? What can you do to change this?

- How can having an eternal view make you more productive in this life?

- What are the practical things you can do this week to live with eternity in mind?

We've Already Won

———————◆◆◆◆◆———————

Movie critics wisely include *spoiler alert* if they're going to reveal the movie's ending. They must walk a fine line between writing enough content to properly critique a movie without telling people how the movie ends.

Spoiler alert: We win. Victory is ours. One of the last verses in the Bible says, "Then I saw 'a new heaven and a new earth,' for the first heaven and the first earth had passed away" (Revelation 21:1). Jesus is already there, waiting to welcome us into eternity. He's gone ahead of us to prepare a place for us (John 14). He's promised incorruptible bodies, perfectly fitted for his heavenly kingdom (1 Corinthians 15). Satan, sin, and sickness will be no more (Revelation 20:11–15).

It's like watching the instant replay of a sporting event in which you know who is going to win the game. On various occasions, I inadvertently found out the winner of the game before watching the replay. If I know my team is going to win, I'm not worried about the outcome when watching the match. Whatever happens during the replay, I know that my team is going to pull it out in the end.

If we really believe that victory awaits us, we don't have to be troubled when problems occur and the situation seems hopeless.

Team Jesus will be victorious. We know how the game turns out. Those who are born again can be confident that God will work all things together for good and he will be the final judge. Paul often helped believers to look at the end game and not get caught up in their current problems. He said to the Corinthians, "For we know that if the earthly tent we live in is destroyed, we have a building from God, an eternal house in heaven, not built by human hands" (2 Corinthians 5:1). He reminded those early Corinthian believers not to worry about circumstances on the earth saying, So we fix our eyes not on what is seen, but on what is unseen, since what is seen is temporary, but what is unseen is eternal" (2 Corinthians 4:17–18).

Keep your eyes on the prize. Reread the book of Revelation. We win.

In 1975, I sang tenor as part of the Shekinah Singers, a large choir directed by Kelly and Lilli Green. Our signature song was the Hallelujah chorus.

And He shall reign forever and ever
Hallelujah! Hallelujah!

That day is right around the corner. The kingdom of this world will soon become the kingdom of our Lord. Hallelujah!

We can rejoice now because of Christ's resurrection victory. His life, death, and resurrection has assured us eternal life and bliss for eternity.

The sting of death will soon be swallowed into life. Paul says, "Where, O death, is your victory? Where, O death, is your sting?" (1 Corinthians 15:55). Even though we know the end and we will reign victoriously with Christ, we need to learn how to live victoriously in this life.

As you apply the truths of this book, you'll stay strong during the journey as you move toward the final victory.

We can trust in his loving control over every circumstance. Nothing escapes his care. Life has a purpose. And his grace covers our sin and shortcoming. The cross is our victory. And even good works are a result of his work of grace. Rather than feeling the constant guilt of "I should have," we need to say, "Lord, help me to know your love for me through Jesus Christ and give me the grace to live for each day."

Spending time in his presence helps us reflect on his sovereign grace. We remember what he has done for us and who we are in Christ. We are no longer pretending to be someone we are not meant to be. During our quiet time each day, he helps us refocus on God and his perfect plan for our lives.

True success is having those closest to us love and respect us the most. Those are the ones who bring out the rough edges and tell us where we need his deeper work of holiness. God has developed his church to help us in the process. Jesus, the head of the church, has created his church here on earth to build up believers. It's a simple church, existing of God-given leadership and a two-winged structure—both large and small groups.

We will be more fruitful if we rest well. All fruitful work comes from deep rest. We neglect a weekly day of rest and regular vacations at our own peril. When running on empty, people notice it. They feel the stress and human pressure. Until we get our new bodies, we are still bound to this earth in human flesh and blood. And the Holy Spirit lives in us! Make him comfortable by eating well, sleeping a lot, and exercising sufficiently.

The good news is that God has given us all the resources we need to live victoriously. He's given us his Holy Spirit to dwell with in, the cross of Christ to cleanse us, and a loving heavenly Father who cares for us. We can declare with the apostle Paul, "But thanks be to God! He gives us the victory through our Lord Jesus Christ" (1 Corinthians 15:57). Victory is ours both in this life and the next one.

Hallelujah! And He shall reign forever and ever. And we will reign with him. Hallelujah!

Appendix

I do better at fulfilling my goals if I'm measuring them. Each day, I write down the number of steps I've taken, hours I've slept, and whether I ate healthy food. Then I average them out on my day off. Here's a random week of my measurements:

Date	Steps	Sleep	Eating
Thursday	14,734	7	10
Friday	16,239	5.75	10
Saturday	14,672	7.75	9
Sunday	14,464	6.25	10
Monday	13,372	6.25	9
Tuesday	12,270	7.25	9
Wednesday		9.5	10
Week Average	14,291	7.1	9.6

The second column, *steps*, shows how many steps I took each day for the entire week. I then divide the total of recorded daily steps by the number of days for which steps were recorded to get the average steps per day for that week. You might have noticed the blank space on Wednesday. I don't measure my steps on my day off because I just want to relax and not worry about how much I walk on that day. However, sleeping and food intake is important to me on my day off, so I do measure them.

The third column is the amount of sleep for each day. If I slept 6 hours and 45 minutes on a particular night, I'll divide the 45 by 60 minutes, which comes to 6.75 hours. With time slept recorded in hours using this decimal numbers formatting, I can then easily get an accurate average of daily hours slept for the entire week. My goal is to get a daily average of 7 hours of sleep.

The fourth column records on a scale of 1 to 10 how well I am meeting my eating plan, which is a more subjective measurement. I score myself according to how well I adhered to my self-imposed eating plan. Even though this is subjective, I've discovered it works well in holding myself accountable.

Notes

1. *Facts & Faith* website, "Joni Eareckson Tada—Diving Accident Renders Her Quadriplegic at 17—Says She Wouldn't Change a Thing," http://factsandfaith.com/joni-eareckson-tada-diving-accident-renders-her-quadriplegic-at-17-says-she-wouldnt-change-a-thing/.

2. Jerry Bridges, *Is God Really in Control? Trusting God in a World of Hurt* (Kindle Locations 259–261), Kindle edition, (NavPress, 2006).

3. *Christianity Today*, "Laura Story on life's difficulties and why she still feels blessed," https://www.christiantoday.com/article/laura.story.on.lifes.difficulties.and.why.she.still.feels.blessed/27814.htm.

4. Jerry Bridges, *Is God Really in Control? Trusting God in a World of Hurt* (Kindle Locations 235–236). Kindle edition, (NavPress, 2006).

5. John Calvin, *Institutes of the Christian Religion* (Grand Rapids, MI: Eerdmans Printing Company, 1983), 194.

6. John Calvin, *Institutes of the Christian Religion,* as quoted on *Christian History Institute*, introduced by Stephen Tomkins, edited for the web by Dan Graves, https://christianhistoryinstitute.org/study/module/calvin-on-gods-sovereignty.

7. Mark R. Talbot, *Suffering and the Sovereignty of God*, ch. 2 "'All the Good That Is Ours in Christ': Seeing God's Gracious Hand in the Hurts Others Do to Us," editors, John Piper and Justin Taylor (Wheaton, Illinois: Crossway Books, 2006), 77.

8. https://www.webtruth.org/christian-history/john-newton-1725-1807.

9. Al Rogers, "Amazing Grace: The Story of John Newton" (reprinted from 1996 article), http://www.reformedreader.org/rbb/newton/amazingrace.htm.

10. http://www.webtruth.org/christian-history/john-newton-1725-1807/.

11. https://www.webtruth.org/christian-history/john-newton-1725-1807.

12. Jerry Bridges, *Transforming Grace,* The Navigators, Kindle edition, 41.

13. C. H. Spurgeon, *The Complete Works of C. H. Spurgeon* (Fort Collins, Colorado: Delmarva Publications, 2013), Volume 60: Sermons 3387–3439.

14. John Stott, *The Cross of Christ* (Downers Grove, Illinois: InterVarsity Press, 1986), 38.

15. PBS video on Martin Luther, https://www.pbs.org/empires/martin luther/char_parents.html.

16. PBS video on Martin Luther, https://www.pbs.org/empires/martin luther/char_parents.html.

17. As quoted in John Stott, *The Cross of Christ* (Downers Grove, Illinois: InterVarsity Press, 1986), 200.

18. Steve McVey, *Grace Walk* (Eugene, Oregon: Harvest House Publishers, 2005), 82.

19. Ibid., 83,

20. Chuck Smith, *Why Grace Changes Everything* (Eugene, Oregon: Harvest House, 1994), 114.

21. J. I. Packer, *Knowing God* (Downer Grove, Illinois: InterVarsity Press, 1973), 34.

22. As quoted in Bruce Wilkinson's, *Secrets of the Vine* (Sisters, OR: Multnomah, 2001), 106.

23. Henry T. Blackaby, Richard Blackaby, and Claude V. King, *Experiencing God* (Nashville: Broadman & Holman, 1994), 2.

24. Henry T. Blackaby, Richard Blackaby, and Claude V. King, *Experiencing God* (Nashville: Broadman & Holman, 1994), 80.

25. LeRoy Eims, *What Every Christian Should Know About Growing* (Wheaton: Victor, 1984), 26.

26. Richard Foster, *Celebration of Discipline* (New York: Harper & Row, 1978), 31.

27. As quoted in *Osvaldo Cruzado*, manual on personal devotions. Originally distributed by the Spanish District of the C&MA in greater New York area.

28. Ibid.

29. Bruce Wilkinson, *Secrets of the Vine* (Sisters, OR: Multnomah, 2001), 101.

30. Frank C. Laubach, *Channels of Spiritual Power* (Los Angeles: Fleming H. Revell, 1954), 95.

31. Paul Cedar, *A Life of Prayer* (Nashville: Word, 1998), 191.

32. *The American Heritage® Dictionary of the English Language*, 3rd ed. copyright ©1992 by Houghton Mifflin Company. Electronic version licensed from INSO Corporation; further reproduction and distribution restricted in accordance with the Copyright Law of the United States. All rights reserved.

33. George Müller, *The Autobiography of George Müller*, Diana L. Matisko, ed., (Springdale, PA.: Whitaker House, 1984), 140.

34. As quoted from https://www.awakenthegreatnesswithin.com/35 -inspirational-quotes-on-journaling.

35. As quoted in Peter Wagner's, *Warfare Prayer* (Ventura, CA: Regal, 1992), 86.

36. Peter Wagner, *Prayer Shield* (Ventura, CA: Regal, 1992), 86.

37. Mark Galli, "Is the Gay Marriage Debate Over?" *Christianity Today,* https://www.christianitytoday.com/ct/2009/july/34.30.html, (July 2009), 33.

38. John Maxwell, "A New Definition of Success" blog post, https://www.johnmaxwell.com/blog/a-new-definition-of-success.

39. Ibid.

40. As quoted in Randy Frazee's, *The Connecting Church* (Grand Rapids: Zondervan, 2001), 13.

41. Mike Mason, *Practicing the Presence of People* (Colorado Springs: Waterbrook Press, 1999), 106.

42. Michael Farris, *What a Daughter Needs from Her Dad* (Minneapolis: Bethany House, 2004), 26.

43. Tod E. Bolsinger, *It Takes a Church to Raise a Christian* (Grand Rapids, MI: Brazos Press, 2004), 71.

44. The church, unlike a normal social gathering, is under the marching orders of Jesus Christ who is the head of the church and its Lord (Ephesians 1:22–23). The church is guided by God-given leadership. Jesus calls specific men and women to guide his church and care for it (Ephesians 4:1–4). We are told by the writer of Hebrews that we are to submit to God-ordained leadership because they watch over our souls and must give an account (Hebrews 13:17). The church participates in the sacraments, which are the Lord's supper (Matthew 26:26–28) and baptism (Matthew 28:18–19). Baptism in water is the entryway or public confession into Christ's church and the Lord's Supper is the remembrance of Christ's death and resurrection (1 Corinthians 11:23–26). God asks us to remember what Jesus has already done for us on the cross. The key here is that he wants us to do this together on a regular basis.

45. Michael J. Wilkins, *Following the Master* (Grand Rapids, MI: Zondervan, 1992), 279.

46. As quoted in Joe Carter's, "Why Christians Don't Go to Church (and Why They Must)" blog post, https://www.thegospelcoalition.org/article/americans-christians-dont-go-church-must.

47. https://www.azquotes.com/quote/697892

48. Robert Banks, *Paul's Idea of Community* (Peabody, MA: Hendrickson Publications, 1994), 49.

49. Joseph Hellerman, *When the Church Was a Family* (Nashville, TN: B&H Academic, 2009), 124.

50. Juliet B. Schor, *The Overworked American: The Unexpected Decline of Leisure* (New York: Basic Books, 1991) as quoted in A. J. Swoboda's: *Subversive*

Sabbath: The Surprising Power of Rest in a Nonstop World (Grand Rapids, Baker Book House), Kindle edition, location 597.

51. Marva J. Dawn, *Keeping the Sabbath Wholly* (Grand Rapids, Michigan: Wm. B. Eerdmans Publishing Co., 1989), 5.

52. A. J., Swoboda: *Subversive Sabbath: The Surprising Power of Rest in a Nonstop World* (Grand Rapids, Baker Book House), Kindle edition, location 2021.

53. As quoted in Emily Mcfarlan Miller's, "The science of Sabbath: How people are rediscovering rest—and claiming its benefits," Religion News Service, https://religionnews.com/transmission/the-science-of-sabbath-how-people-are-rediscovering-rest-and-claiming-its-benefits (requires a subscription).

54. Marva J. Dawn, *Keeping the Sabbath Wholly* (Grand Rapids, Michigan: Wm. B. Eerdmans Publishing Co., 1989), 7.

55. Chuck Bentley, "What Does the Bible Say About Taking Vacations?" (Christian Post, September 15, 2007), https://www.christianpost.com/news/ask-chuck-what-does-the-bible-say-about-taking-vacations.html.

56. Will Maule, "5 Reasons It Is Biblical To Take A Vacation," https://hellochristian.com/3308-5-reasons-it-is-biblical-to-take-a-vacation.

57. Irenaeus, *Against Heresies,* https://earlychurchtexts.com/public/image_and_likeness.htm.

58. John Piper, "How Much Does God Want Me to Care for My Physical Body?" blog post, https://www.desiringgod.org/interviews/how-much-does-god-want-me-to-care-for-my-physical-body.

59. Jeremy Bell, "Christian, Take Care of Your Body" blog post, http://intersectproject.org/faith-and-culture/christian-take-care-body.

60. Jenna Fletcher, *MedicalNewsToday*, reviewed by Deborah Weatherspoon, PhD, RN, CRNA on May 31, 2019, https://www.medicalnewstoday.com/articles/325353.php#greater-athletic-performance. The National Sleep Foundation suggests that adults need between seven and nine hours a night and athletes may benefit from as many as ten hours. The body heals during sleep. Other benefits include better performance intensity, more energy, better coordination, faster speed, and better mental functioning.

61. Unhealthy eating habits have contributed to the obesity epidemic in the United States where about one-third of U.S. adults (33.8 percent) are obese and approximately 17 percent (or 12.5 million) of children and adolescents aged 2–19 years are obese (U.S. Department of Health and Human Services), https://www.hhs.gov/fitness/eat-healthy/importance-of-good-nutrition/index.html.

62. Since 2006, I had generally followed Joel Fuhrman's "Life Plan" from his book *Eat to Live* (https://www.amazon.com/Eat-Live-Amazing-Nutrient-Rich-Sustained-ebook/dp/B0047Y175M/)

But I had also taken many more eating liberties than necessary. I lacked the discipline to get back on his general plan after a conference. Losing weight, according to Fuhrman, was the byproduct of healthy eating. Fuhrman points to many scientific studies to support an emphasis on plant-based foods. Fuhrman is against diets and views healthy eating as the best way to avoid disease, while losing weight as a result. Fuhrman's life plan includes some meat and dairy, but he emphasizes fruits, salads, vegetables, and legumes. He also has a six-week plan for those getting started, which I followed for six-weeks back in 2006. Since then I had generally tried to stay on his life plan with some success. In January 2019, I decided to follow the six-week plan and stay on it indefinitely. Staying faithful to Fuhrman's six-week plan was hard because of my travel schedule, but I decided to give it a try. I had to explain to host churches that I was only going to eat certain foods, such as fruits, vegetables, salads, legumes, nuts, and other plant-based foods. In explaining my new diet to these churches, I normally just mentioned my high cholesterol without going into a lot more detail. As a result of this plan, I lost twenty-five pounds and have kept those pounds off for one year. I have felt a lot more energy in everything I do. For example, at my wife's yearly family camp in August 2019, I played several rounds of basketball without becoming exhausted, something I could not do in 2018 on the same court and with many of the same people.

63. I've read and reread *Eat to Live* for a long time. However, one caution about Fuhrman's writing is his critical attitude. He often uses harsh, judgmental language to describe diets and foods he doesn't recommend. He repeatedly describes normal food, like dairy products, as cancer producing. I started reading Fuhrman in 2006 and had to eventually stop reading the book because I found myself becoming critical of my children who were eating a normal, North American diet. I often placed a guilt trip on them and had to repent of my judgmental attitude. I've learned to back off and give people liberty to make their own eating decisions.

64. The study analyzed the responses of 123,216 people with no history of prior disease. These participants were followed for fourteen years, from 1993 to 2006. The study concluded, "After adjusting for a number of risk factors, . . . women who spent six hours a day sitting had a 37 percent increased risk of dying versus those who spent less than three hours a day on their bottoms. For men the increased risk was 17 percent. (See Amanda Gardner, "The Longer You Sit, the Shorter Your Life Span: Study," July 22, 2010, https://consumer.healthday.com/cancer-information-5/mis-cancer-news-102/the-longer-you-sit-the-shorter-your-life-span-study-641401.html).

65. Paige Waehner, "Everything You Need to Know About Cardio," medically reviewed by Tara Laferrara, CPT (October 31, 2019), https://www.verywellfit.com/everything-you-need-to-know-about-cardio-1229553.

66. Joshua Bote, "Do you really need to walk 10,000 steps a day?" https://www.usatoday.com/story/news/nation/2020/01/04/walking-10-000-steps-day-good-fitness-goal-heres-better-one/2784372001. According to this article, it's great if a person can walk 10,000 steps daily, and this is great advice for younger people or those who have more experience with a fitness regimen. But for older people and those who are less fit, 10,000 steps per day can be demoralizing. For those who are inactive, setting too high of a standard may discourage them from exercising entirely.

67. As quoted in Gretchen Rubin's, "If You Want to Achieve a Goal, Measure Your Progress" blog post on *HuffPost*, (December 3, 2010, updated November 17, 2011), https://www.huffpost.com/entry/balanced-life-

68. As quoted in https://en.wikipedia.org/wiki/Charles_Studd

69. Ibid.

70. Randy Alcorn, *Heaven* (Carol Stream, Illinois: Tyndale House Publishers, 2009), Kindle locations 285–290.

71. John Chrysostom, as quoted in https://biblehub.com/commentaries/chrysostom/2_corinthians/5.htm.

72. John Blanchard, *Does God Believe in Atheists?* (Evangelical Press, 2000), Kindle edition, location 3100.

73. Ibid., location 3100.

74. Dietrich Bonhoeffer, "German theologian and resister," *Christianity Today* (January 2020), https://www.christianitytoday.com/history/people/martyrs/dietrich-bonhoeffer.html.

Resources

by
Joel Comiskey

**You can find all of Joel Comiskey's books at
Joel Comiskey Group
Phone: 1-888-511-9995
Website: www.joelcomiskeygroup.com**

Joel Comiskey's previous books cover the following topics

- Leading a cell group (*How to Lead a Great Cell Group Meeting*, 2001, 2009; *Children in Cell Ministry*, 2015; *Youth in Cell Ministry*, 2016; *Groups that Thrive*, 2018; *Facilitate*, 2019).

- How to multiply the cell group (*Home Cell Group Explosion*, 1998).

- How to prepare spiritually for cell ministry (*An Appointment with the King*, 2002, 2011).

- How to practically organize your cell system (*Reap the Harvest*, 1999; *Cell Church Explosion*, 2004).

- How to train future cell leaders (*Leadership Explosion*, 2001; *Live*, 2007; *Encounter*, 2007; *Grow*, 2007; *Share*, 2007; *Lead*, 2007; *Coach*, 2008; *Discover*, 2008).

- How to coach/care for cell leaders (*How to be a Great Cell Group Coach*, 2003; *Groups of Twelve*, 2000; *From Twelve to Three*, 2002).

- How the gifts of the Spirit work within the cell group (*The Spirit-filled Small Group*, 2005, 2009; *Discover*, 2008).

- How to fine tune your cell system (*Making Cell Groups Work Navigation Guide*, 2003).

- Principles from the second largest church in the world (*Passion and Persistence*, 2004).

- How cell church works in North America (*The Church that Multiplies*, 2007, 2009).

- How to plant a church (*Planting Churches that Reproduce*, 2009)

- How to be a relational disciple (*Relational Disciple*, 2010).

- How to distinguish truth from myths (*Myths and Truths of the Cell Church*, 2011).

- What the Biblical foundations for cell church are (*Biblical Foundations for the Cell-Based Church*, 2012, *Making Disciples in the Cell-Based Church*, 2013, 2000 Years of Small Groups, 2015).

All of the books listed are available from Joel Comiskey Group

www.joelcomiskeygroup.com

How To Lead a Great Cell Group Meeting: So People Want to Come Back

Do people expectantly return to your group meetings every week? Do you have fun and experience joy during your meetings? Is everyone participating in discussion and ministry? You can lead a great cell group meeting, one that is life changing and dynamic. Most people don't realize that they can create a God-filled atmosphere because they don't know how. Now the secret is out. This guide will show you how to:

▢ Prepare yourself spiritually to hear God during the meeting

▢ Structure the meeting so it flows

▢ Spur people in the group to participate and share their lives openly

▢ Share your life with others in the group

▢ Create stimulating questions

▢ Listen effectively to discover what is transpiring in others' lives

▢ Encourage and edify group members

▢ Open the group to non-Christians

▢ See the details that create a warm atmosphere

By implementing these time-tested ideas, your group meetings will become the hot-item of your members' week. They will go home wanting more and return each week bringing new people with them. 140 pgs.

Home Cell Group Explosion: How Your Small Group Can Grow and Multiply

The book crystallizes the author's findings in some eighteen areas of research, based on a meticulous questionnaire that he submitted to cell church leaders in eight countries around the world, locations that he also visited personally for his research. The detailed notes in the back of the book offer the student of cell church growth a rich mine for further reading. The beauty of Comiskey's book is that he not only summarizes his survey results in a thoroughly convincing way but goes on to analyze in practical ways many of his survey results in separate chapters. The happy result is that any cell church leader, intern or member completing this quick read will have his priorities/values clearly aligned and ready to be followed-up. If you are a pastor or small group leader, you should devour this book! It will encourage you and give you simple, practical steps for dynamic small group life and growth. 175 pgs.

An Appointment with the King: *Ideas for Jump-Starting Your Devotional Life*

With full calendars and long lists of things to do, people often put on hold life's most important goal: building an intimate relationship with God. Often, believers wish to pursue the goal but are not sure how to do it. They feel frustrated or guilty when their attempts at personal devotions seem empty and unfruitful. With warm, encouraging writing, Joel Comiskey guides readers on how to set a daily appointment with the King and make it an exciting time they will look forward to. This book first answers the question "Where do I start?" with step-by-step instructions on how to spend time with God and practical ideas for experiencing him more fully. Second, it highlights the benefits of spending time with God, including joy, victory over sin, and spiritual guidance. The book will help Christians tap into God's resources on a daily basis, so that even in the midst of busyness they can walk with him in intimacy and abundance. 175 pgs.

Reap the Harvest: *How a Small Group System Can Grow System Can Grow Your Church*

Have you tried small groups and hit a brick wall? Have you wondered why your groups are not producing the fruit that was promised? Are you looking to make your small groups more effective? Cell-church specialist and pastor Dr. Joel Comiskey studied the world's most successful cell churches to determine why they grow. The key: They have embraced specific principles. Conversely, churches that do not embrace these same principles have problems with their groups and therefore do not grow. Cell churches are successful not because they have small groups but because they can support the groups. In this book, you will discover how these systems work. 236 pgs.

La Explosión de la Iglesia Celular: *Cómo Estructurar la Iglesia en Células Eficaces (Editorial Clie, 2004)*

This book is available only in Spanish and contains Joel Comiskey's research of eight of the world's largest cell churches, five of which reside in Latin America. It details how to make the transition from a traditional church to the cell church structure and many other valuable insights, including: the history of the cell church, how to organize your church to become a praying church, the most important principles of the cell church, and how to raise up an army of cell leaders. 236 pgs.

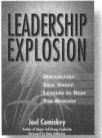

Leadership Explosion: *Multiplying Cell Group Leaders to Reap the Harvest*

Some have said that cell groups are leader breeders. Yet even the best cell groups often have a leadership shortage. This shortage impedes growth and much of the harvest goes untouched. Joel Comiskey has discovered why some churches are better at raising up new cell leaders than others. These churches do more than pray and hope for new leaders. They have an intentional strategy, a plan that will quickly equip as many new leaders as possible. In this book, you will discover the training models these churches use to multiply leaders. You will discover the underlying principles of these models so that you can apply them. 202 pgs.

FIVE-BOOK EQUIPPING SERIES

| #1: Live | #2: Encounter | #3: Grow | #4: Share | #5: Lead |

The five book equipping series is designed to train a new believer all the way to leading his or her own cell group. Each of the five books contains eight lessons. Each lesson has interactive activities that helps the trainee reflect on the lesson in a personal, practical way.

Live starts the training by covering key Christian doctrines, including baptism and the Lord's supper. 85 pgs.

Encounter guides the believer to receive freedom from sinful bondages. The *Encounter* book can be used one-on-one or in a group. 91 pgs.

Grow gives step-by-step instruction for having a daily quiet time, so that the believer will be able to feed him or herself through spending daily time with God. 87 pgs.

Share instructs the believer how to communicate the gospel message in a winsome, personal way. This book also has two chapters on small group evangelism. 91 pgs.

Lead prepares the Christian on how to facilitate an effective cell group. This book would be great for those who form part of a small group team. 91 pgs.

TWO-BOOK ADVANCED TRAINING SERIES

Coach   Discover

Coach and *Discover* make-up the Advanced Training, prepared specifically to take a believer to the next level of maturity in Christ.

Coach prepares a believer to coach another cell leader. Those experienced in cell ministry often lack understanding on how to coach someone else. This book provides step-by-step instruction on how to coach a new cell leader from the first meeting all the way to giving birth to a new group. The book is divided into eight lessons, which are interactive and help the potential coach deal with real-life, practical coaching issues. 85 pgs.

Discover clarifies the twenty gifts of the Spirit mentioned in the New Testament. The second part shows the believer how to find and use his or her particular gift. This book is excellent to equip cell leaders to discover the giftedness of each member in the group. 91 pgs.

How to be a Great Cell Group Coach: Practical insight for Supporting and Mentoring Cell Group Leaders

Research has proven that the greatest contributor to cell group success is the quality of coaching provided for cell group leaders. Many are serving in the position of a coach, but they don't fully understand what they are supposed to do in this position. Joel Comiskey has identified seven habits of great cell group coaches. These include: Receiving from God, Listening to the needs of the cell group leader, Encouraging the cell group leader, Caring for the multiple aspects of a leader's life, Developing the cell leader in various aspects of leadership, Strategizing with the cell leader to create a plan, Challenging the cell leader to grow.

Practical insights on how to develop these seven habits are outlined in section one. Section two addresses how to polish your skills as a coach with instructions on diagnosing problems in a cell group, how to lead coaching meetings, and what to do when visiting a cell group meeting. This book will prepare you to be a great cell group coach, one who mentors, supports, and guides cell group leaders into great ministry. 139 pgs.

Groups of Twelve: A New Way to Mobilize Leaders and Multiply Groups in Your Church

This book clears the confusion about the Groups of 12 model. Joel dug deeply into the International Charismatic Mission in Bogota, Colombia and other G12 churches to learn the simple principles that G12 has to offer your church. This book also contrasts the G12 model with the classic 5x5 and shows you what to do with this new model of ministry. Through onsite research, international case studies, and practical experience, Joel Comiskey outlines the G12 principles that your church can use today.

Billy Hornsby, director of the Association of Related Churches, says, "Joel Comiskey shares insights as a leader who has himself raised up numerous leaders. From how to recognize potential leaders to cell leader training to time-tested principles of leadership this book has it all. The accurate comparisons of various training models make it a great resource for those who desire more leaders. Great book!" 182 pgs.

From Twelve To Three: *How to Apply G12 Principles in Your Church*

The concept of the Groups of 12 began in Bogota, Colombia, but now it is sweeping the globe. Joel Comiskey has spent years researching the G12 structure and the principles behind it.

From his experience as a pastor, trainer, and consultant, he has discovered that there are two ways to embrace the G12 concept: adopting the entire model or applying the principles that support the model.

This book focuses on the application of principles rather than adoption of the entire model. It outlines the principles and provides a modified application which Joel calls the G12.3. This approach presents a pattern that is adaptable to many different church contexts.

The concluding section illustrates how to implement the G12.3 in various kinds of churches, including church plants, small churches, large churches, and churches that already have cells. 178 pgs.

The Spirit-filled Small Group: Leading Your Group to Experience the Spiritual Gifts

The focus in many of today's small groups has shifted from Spirit-led transformation to just another teacher-student Bible study. But exercising every member's spiritual gifts is vital to the effectiveness of the group. With insight born of experience in more than twenty years of small group ministry, Joel Comiskey explains how leaders and participants alike can be supernaturally equipped to deal with real-life issues. Put these principles into practice and your small group will never be the same!

This book works well with Comiskey's training book, **Discover.** It fleshes out many of the principles in Comiskey's training book. Chuck Crismier, radio host, *Viewpoint,* writes, ⬭Joel Comiskey has again provided the Body of Christ with an important tool to see God's Kingdom revealed in and through small groups.⬭ 191 pgs.

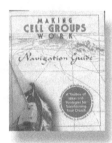

Making Cell Groups Work Navigation Guide: A Toolbox of Ideas and Strategies for Transforming Your Church

For the first time, experts in cell group ministry have come together to provide you with a page reference tool like no other. When Ralph Neighbour, Bill Beckham, Joel Comiskey and Randall Neighbour compiled new articles and information under careful orchestration and in-depth understanding that Scott Boren brings to the table, it's as powerful as private consulting! Joel Comiskey has an entire book within this mammoth page work. There are also four additional authors.

Passion and Persistence: How the Elim Church's Cell Groups Penetrated an Entire City for Jesus

This book describes how the Elim Church in San Salvador grew from a small group to 116,000 people in 10,000 cell groups. Comiskey takes the principles from Elim and applies them to churches in North America and all over the world. Ralph Neighbour says: "I believe this book will be remember as one of the most important ever written about a cell church movement! I experienced the passion when visiting Elim many years ago. Comiskey's report about Elim is not a pattern to be slavishly copied. It is a journey into grasping the true theology and methodology of the New Testament church. You'll discover how the Elim Church fans into flame their passion for Jesus and His Word, how they organize their cells to penetrate a city and world for Jesus, and how they persist until God brings the fruit." 158 pgs.

The Church that Multiplies: Growing a Healthy Cell Church in North America

Does the cell church strategy work in North America? We hear about exciting cell churches in Colombia and Korea, but where are the dynamic North American cell churches? This book not only declares that the cell church concept does work in North America but dedicates an entire chapter to examining North American churches that are successfully using the cell strategy to grow in quality and quantity. This book provides the latest statistical research about the North American church and explains why the cell church approach restores health and growth to the church today. More than anything else, this book will provide practical solutions for pastors and lay leaders to use in implementing cell-based ministry. 181 pgs.

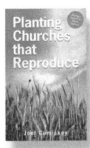

Planting Churches that Reproduce: Planting a Network of Simple Churches

What is the best way to plant churches in the 21st century? Comiskey believes that simple, reproducible church planting is most effective. The key is to plant churches that are simple enough to grow into a movement of churches. Comiskey has been gathering material for this book for the past fifteen Years. He has also planted three churches in a wide variety of settings. Planting Churches that Reproduce is the fruit of his research and personal experience. Comiskey uses the latest North American church planting statistics, but extends the illustrations to include worldwide church planting. More than anything else, this book will provide practical solutions for those planting churches today. Comiskey's book is a must-read book for all those interested in establishing Christ-honoring, multiplying churches. 176 pgs.

The Relational Disciple: How God Uses Community to Shape Followers of Jesus

Jesus lived with His disciples for three years and taught them life lessons as a group. After three years, he commanded them to go and do likewise (Matthew 28:18-20). Jesus discipled His followers through relationships and He wants us to do the same. Scripture is full of exhortations to love and serve one another. This book will show you how. The isolation present in the western world is creating a hunger for community and the world is longing to see relational disciples in action. This book will encourage Christ-followers to allow God to use the natural relationships in life family, friends, work relationships, cells, church, and missions to mold them into relational disciples.

You Can Coach: *How to Help Leaders Build Healthy Churches through Coaching*

We've entitled this book "You Can Coach" because we believe that coaching is more about passing on what you've lived and holding others accountable in the process. Coaching doesn't require a higher degree, special talent, unique personality, or a particular spiritual gift. We believe, in fact, that God wants coaching to become a movement. We long to see the day in which every pastor has a coach and in turn is coaching someone else. In this book, you'll hear three coaches who have successfully coached pastors for many years. They will share their history, dreams, principles, and what God is doing through coaching. Our hope is that you'll be both inspired and resourced to continue your own coaching ministry in the years to come.

Myths & Truths of the Cell Church: *Key Principles that Make or Break Cell Ministry*

Most of the modern day cell church movement is dynamic, positive, and applicable. As is true in most endeavors, errors and false assumptions have also cropped up to destroy an otherwise healthy movement. Sometimes these false concepts caused the church to go astray completely. At other times, they led the pastor and church down a dead-end road of fruitless ministry. Regardless of how the myths were generated, they had a chilling effect on the church's ministry. In this book, Joel Comiskey tackles these errors and false assumptions, helping pastors and leaders to untangle the webs of legalism that has crept into the cell church movement. Joel then guides the readers to apply biblical, time-tested principles that will guide them into fruitful cell ministry. Each chapter begins with a unique twist. Well-known worldwide cell church leaders open each chapter by answering questions to the chapter's topic in the form of an email dialogue. Whether you're starting out for the first time in cell ministry or a seasoned veteran, this book will give you the tools to help your ministry stay fresh and fruitful.

Biblical Foundations for the Cell-Based Church

Why cell church? Is it because David Cho's church is a cell church and happens to be the largest church in the history of Christianity? Is it because cell church is the strategy that many "great" churches are using?

Ralph Neighbour repeatedly says, "Theology must breed methodology." Joel Comiskey has arrived at the same conclusion. Biblical truth is the only firm foundation for anything we do. Without a biblical base, we don't have a strong under-pinning upon which we can hang our ministry and philosophy. We can plod through most anything when we know that God is stirring us to behave biblically.

Making Disciples in the Cell-Based Church

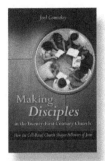

The primary goal of the church is to make disciples who make disciples. But how is the church supposed to do that? This book answers that question. Dr. Comiskey explains how both cell and celebration (larger gathering) work together in the process of making disciples. In the cell, a potential disciple is transformed through community, priesthood of all believers, group evangelism, and team multiplication. The cell system ensures each leader has a coach and that training happens. Then the cells gather together to worship and grow through the teaching of God's Word. This book will help you understand why and how to become a church that prioritizes discipleship.

What others are saying: I've read all of Joel Comiskey's books, but this one is his best work yet. I'm looking forward to having all of our pastors, coaches, cell leaders and members read this book in the near future. *Dr. Dennis Watson, Lead Pastor, Celebration Church of New Orleans*

I am so excited about Joel Comiskey's new book, Making Disciples in the Twenty-First Century Church. Joel has unpacked discipleship, not just as an endeavor for individuals, but as the critical element for creating a church community and culture that reproduces the Kingdom of God all over the earth. *Jimmy Seibert, Senior Pastor, Antioch Community Church*

Like Joel's other books, this one is solidly biblical, highly practical, wonderfully accessible and is grounded in Joel's vast research and experience. *Dr. Dave Earley, Lead Pastor, Grace City Church of Las Vegas, Nevada*

2000 Years of Small Groups:
A History of Cell Ministry in the Church

This book explores how God has used small groups throughout church history, specifically focusing on the early church to the present time. God not only established the early church as a house to house movement, but he also has used small groups throughout church history. This book chronicles the small group or cell movement from Jesus all the way to the modern day cell explosion. Themes include:Small Groups In Biblical History, Small Groups In Early Christian History, Small Groups and Monasticism, Small Groups During the Pre-Reformation Period, Luther and Small Groups, Martin Bucer and Small Groups, The Anabaptist Movement, Puritan Conventicles, Pietism, The Moravians, The Methodists, Modern House Churches, Small Groups in North America, and The Modern Day Cell Church. This book will both critique the strengths and weaknesses of these historical movements and apply principles to today's church.

Children in Cell Ministry:
Discipling the Future Generation Now

Joel Comiskey challenges pastors and leaders to move from simply educating children to forming them into disciples who make disciples. Comiskey lays out the Biblical base for children's ministry and then encourages pastors and leaders to formulate their own vision and philosophy for ministry to children based on the Biblical text. Comiskey highlights how to disciple children in both the large group and the small group. He quickly moves into practical examples of intergenerational cell groups and how effective cell churches have implemented this type of group. He then writes about children only cell groups, citing many practical examples from some of the most effective cell churches in the world. Comiskey covers equipping for children, how to equip the parents, and mistakes in working with children in the cell church. This book will help those wanting to minister to children both in large and small groups.

Groups that Thrive

Why are some small groups dynamic, attractive, and breathe the life of Christ? Why do other groups stagnate and close? In this ground-breaking book, Joel Comiskey and Jim Egli describe eight surprises about thriving small groups from their research of 4800 small group participants on four continents.

The authors expose common small group assumptions and offer practical advice to group members and leaders to help their groups thrive. The book covers topics such as small group participation, the influence of food, worship, and how thriving small groups effectively reach others for Jesus Christ. Read this book if you want your group to grow healthier and thrive with new life.

Facilitate

Facilitate highlights the key dynamics of small groups that will give a leader confidence to minister to those in the group. Facilitate teaches a leader how to listen well, ask questions, train others, involve people, and prepare for the meeting. This book shows a potential leader how to develop new leaders to continue the discipleship process. It is excellent to use both in a Sunday school class and one on one. This book has eight lessons, full of practical questions and applications. You will learn how to:-Prepare spiritually for the power of God to flow in the meeting-Structure the meeting in a dynamic and effective way-Encourage attendees to participate and share their experiences-Suggest interesting topics and questions-Listen carefully and detect problems in the groupBy putting into practice the ideas and suggestions in this book, any leader of a cell group will find it easy to achieve an exciting atmosphere in the meetings and ensure that attendees want to come back and even bring new people with them

CPSIA information can be obtained
at www.ICGtesting.com
Printed in the USA
BVHW060218110720
583297BV00007B/27